TRICIA GUILD'S
NEW SOFT FURNISHINGS

TEXT BY TRICIA GUILD AND ELIZABETH WILHIDE

SPECIAL PHOTOGRAPHY BY DAVID MONTGOMERY

CONRAN OCTOPUS

For Lily

I would like to thank Sheila and Chris Halsey
for kindly allowing me to photograph the nursery,
Lesley Harle for designing the book case-cloth and Jo Willer
for her invaluable support, help and encouragement.

Project Editor Joanna Bradshaw   *Art Editor* Meryl Lloyd
Editor Michelle Clark   *Illustrator* Paul Bryant
Production Julia Golding   *Visualizer* Jean Morley
Picture Research Jessica Walton

First published in 1990 by
Conran Octopus Limited
37 Shelton Street, London WC2H 9HN

Reprinted 1991, 1992 (twice)

British Library Cataloguing in Publication Data
Guild, Tricia
    Tricia Guild's new soft furnishings.
    1. Soft furnishings
    I. Title
    646.21

ISBN 1 85029 246 9

Typeset by Hunters Armley Limited
Printed in Hong Kong by Wing King Tong Co. Ltd.

Contents

Introduction 9

Windows 29

Cushions 49

Seating 63

Tables 73

Beds 83

Accessories 105

Stitch Directory and Techniques 115

Fabric Glossary 122

List of Suppliers 124

Index 126

Introduction

Soft furnishings rely on the interplay of colours, textures, patterns and styles in order to create an original look. A successful combination of these elements can be exciting and innovative, with the fabric dressing the room. For a time the term 'soft furnishings' seemed to conjure up a picture of a fussy, overly feminine room, swathed in floral prints and with frilly cushions and flounces. But there is no more reason to choose such fabric treatments for your home than there is to wear a flowery frock if you feel more comfortable wearing a tailored-suit. The scope of soft furnishings is as great as your imagination allows: from sharp, strong modern effects with neat-edged blinds and piped upholstery, or classically elegant drapery requiring more originality than technical expertise, to the most professionally executed curtains, pelmets and tie-backs for a traditional or period room.

Creating a comfortable and original interior need not call for a high level of sewing skills. Often, a complete transformation can be achieved by using simple draping techniques and a careful juxtaposition of different fabrics.

It is a fascinating and rewarding time for those interested in fabric and fabric effects. More colours, more patterns and more types of fabric are available than ever before, and the scope and potential for creativity is greatly increased. Pattern mixing is an excellent strategy for contemporary decorating. It is no longer necessary to select just one design or to combine one pattern with a small-scale version of itself. Traditional chintzes go with checks and stripes, florals with geometrics. With experiment, you can achieve a great sense of vitality.

Inspiration

The collage of photographs on the following pages (14-19), is designed to give some idea of how different colours, textures and patterns can stimulate the imagination. These pictures represent my selection of some of the images which I find invigorating and appealing. Nature is always a powerful influence: fallen leaves, fruit piled on a market stall, fields, seed-heads. Architecture, both grand and vernacular, is equally stimulating as are details such as doorways, architraves and mouldings, tiled floor patterns and roofs. Travel is a very good way of opening your eyes, both to extraordinary sights and to the everyday, which is often overlooked at home.

A collection of similar images – postcards, photographs, magazine clippings – can help you to form your own colour and design sense. Experiment with different groupings and observe the dynamics of different combinations. As an example of this principle, turn to page 19 and cover the picture of the hortensia (second row, second from right) with your hand. The entire composition looks different without the vivid pink accent. Imagine what the page would look like if the picture were yellow, or red. The pink hortensia acts as an accent in the same way as cushions or a table-cloth would in a room. By changing these accessories you can change the whole emphasis of a decorative scheme.

Colour, Texture and Pattern

There are no rules for choosing and using fabric successfully in the interior. In fact, some of the most exciting fabric effects are daring and unconventional.

The biggest mistake most people make in decorating is to be too hesitant. Lack of confidence in your own taste often leads to solutions which are safe and acceptable but also bland and boring.

The first step is to take the fear out of decorating. The way to do this is to get to know what really pleases you, in terms of colour, texture and pattern. It can be quite challenging to abandon notions of what is 'proper and appropriate' or 'good taste' and rediscover the elements which inspire strong positive responses.

Teach yourself to really look at your surroundings and decide what options appeal to you. Keep a scrapbook or file of postcards, scraps of fabric, cuttings from magazines, ribbon, braid, packaging – anything which catches your eye. Before long, you are bound to detect some kind of common denominator. It may be a favourite colour, a particular type of graphic pattern or simply a mood or image which awakens your imagination. There's no need to be self-conscious about this process of 're-education' it can be fun as well as instructive. After all, the whole aim of decorating should be to please yourself, to give a lift to your surroundings which will continue to refresh and delight you.

Colour is one of the most personal elements of all, and the most immediate. Although there are all sorts of accepted views about what colour can do – enlarge space or enclose it, for example – ultimately it is your own personal preferences which matter. If you find yourself really drawn to a particular shade, try to use it in your decorating. Again, most people play safe with colour in the home and miss out on the excitement that colour can bring.

Colours vary according to how they are used; the texture of the surface, how they are combined with other shades, whether they are viewed by artificial or natural light and many other factors. In some contexts, blues can be formal and rather chilly, but they can also be fresh and uplifting. Reds are often dramatic and dominant, but they can also be full of depth and richness. Greens are traditionally restful but they can also take on a refined, elegant look. It takes practice to develop a good eye for colour; at the outset it may be helpful to think in terms of colour families, assembling related shades around a central colour, and then experimenting with contrasts.

Fabric is a very direct way of adding colour to a room, but it is also one of the most important means of introducing an element which can be rather neglected – texture. In a monochromatic or no-colour scheme, textural differences are essential; where there is a variety of colours and patterns, texture provides depth and extra dimension. The appeal of many fabrics is largely based on their textural properties: the sheen of glazed cotton, the roughness of ethnic weaves, the crispness of fine linen, the sensuousness of silk and delicacy of lace. One of the reasons why natural materials are so intrinsically attractive is that they tend to vary texturally.

When people consider fabric, they often think in terms of pattern and this is undoubtedly fabric's main attraction as an element in interior decoration. Pattern is enriching. It supplies rhythm, movement, depth and imagery. A delight in patterns and pattern-making can be found in every culture and at every period of civilization. As with colour, people often find themselves drawn to a particular type of pattern: florals or abstracts, geometrics or traditional motifs. Stripes and checks are very much in the ascendancy at the moment, reflecting a move away from nostalgia and a new interest in a tailored look.

The variety of patterned fabrics available today is immense. Period revivals have ensured that prints from the past remain in production. A new interest in craftwork has helped to inspire many fresh exciting designs with a more modern flavour, while bold ethnic weaves and patterns are also widely available.

But responding to pattern in fabric is only part of the story. Everything in the interior makes a pattern: the way objects or pictures are arranged, the disposition of furniture and table settings. Pattern is not applied to a blank background, it must be seen as integral.

Using Fabric

Once you have begun to develop your own taste and discover your true preferences, the next step is to carry your ideas through into practice. People often instinctively make a good choice and then back away from it, rationalizing themselves out of what would have been exciting and unusual. Of course, not everything works, but strong ideas applied wholeheartedly are rarely the disasters people expect them to be. For example, conventional decorating wisdom maintains that it is best to avoid using fabric on walls in small spaces, in case the overall effect is too claustrophobic and stifling. But I chose to line the walls of a tiny bedroom in a vivid floral print and the result was warm and welcoming rather than cluttered and complicated.

Similarly, there are accepted guidelines as to which type of fabric can be used in which way: a certain weight for curtains, appropriate weaves for upholstery and so on. Obviously, common sense will tell you that a sofa which is going to receive a great deal of wear should not be covered in a pale silk, and that filmy muslin curtains will not do in a room where you need to have some privacy.

Fabric is just one of the elements in decoration, but it has the great advantage of versatility, a quality which I prize very highly. Interior decoration, to me, is the art of arrangement, the creation of unity and harmony. The aim is not to create a set-piece or tableau but a lively, flowing composition, and fabric is a vital part of this process.

Although there are no real rules in decoration, it is possible to ruin a fabric effect by skimping. Fabric must be used generously, to emphasize its innate qualities of movement, its weight and its tactile properties. If you cannot afford enough fabric to make a particular treatment, such as full, gathered curtains with pelmet and tie-backs, change the idea rather than scale down the quantity of material required. When making curtains, use as much fabric as instructions recommend for the width and express a sense of abundance by adding a little extra fabric to the recommended length. Above all, do not settle for a compromise. Wait until you can achieve what you really want rather than make do with a second best which will always jar.

Natural History

*Many Designers Guild collections have their
starting point in nature, either nature on a grand
scale, as in the changing landscape, or nature
close at hand in the garden. Lilacs, roses,
geraniums, hollyhocks and anenomes are just
some of the flowers which have been translated
into prints. To recapture the luminosity and
transparency of petals and leaves, patterns are
designed first in watercolour on a white
background before being produced in cloth.*

Travellers' Tales

*Other cultures, other countries and other times
also supply a wealth of design ideas. Italy,
particularly the decoration of Palladian villas,
has had an enormous impact on the range in
recent years. Frescoes, marbled paper, ceramics
and architectural detail have all provided
memorable images. Old 'documents' – examples of
historical fabrics – can also be studied and
adapted for contemporary use.*

Artists' Ideas

The third, and perhaps most stimulating source of pattern ideas are artists in other fields, either working in collaboration or designing prints themselves, notably the painter Howard Hodgkin, the ceramicist Janice Tchalenko and the artist Kaffe Fassett. Pattern-making is a subtle and complex art. A design often starts with an idea for an image or motif, an idea which can be inspired by any one of a number of things – by the natural world, architecture, ethnic designs, and so on. This central image must then be translated into a 'repeat', duplicated over and over against a background.

Pattern Dynamics

The dynamic of any pattern consists of the way the main image relates to its background: the scale of the design, the balance of colours and the nature of the background itself are the main variables. A strong main image often works better with a patterned background, hence the continuing success of classic prints which combine floral motifs with stripes, or trellis with leaf shapes, for example. Using self-patterned textured material, such as damask, is another way of providing that vital extra dimension.

Colour and Pattern

Vivid, natural colours occur in many Designers Guild collections. The images on this page demonstrate how the colours blue and green, although traditionally held to be a bad colour combination, can and do complement each other very well. The naturally occuring juxtaposition of green-leaved trees against a bright blue sky has been carefully recreated in several recent fabrics. By incorporating soft blue shades with green floral and plant motifs, a soft, naturalistic atmosphere can be created in any interior.

Designing with Flowers

Flowers offer both inspiration and beauty when it comes to soft furnishings. Used in textile design for several centuries, flowers provide countless colours and forms for an enormous variety of floral patterns and motifs, from the simple floral sprigs applied to eighteenth-century American Colonial fabric designs to bright, naturalistic Edwardian chintzes. Fresh flowers placed in a variety of vases add vitality to any room, creating a welcoming ambience and echoing floral fabrics in colour, texture and pattern.

The styles of the past – both in terms of fabric designs and the way different fabrics were used – are a tremendous source of inspiration. Important national collections, such as the Victoria and Albert Museum in London, provide hours of fascinating study; historical houses and a wealth of excellent books and magazines make the subject accessible to everyone. For me, history is a starting point; I can appreciate that for some people it is very important to reproduce a period interior down to the last detail, but I tend to look at the past as just one of many influences and sources of inspiration.

Patterned Bedside

right *Pattern mixing is just as evident in period decoration as it is in today's homes. This bedside corner, with bolster, bed curtain and cover all in different fabrics, displays a subtle and sophisticated blend of colours and designs that work well together.*

French Neo-classicism

above *France at the end of the eighteenth century was a centre of excellence in the field of upholstery and furnishing. The fabrics and fabric treatments were at a peak of refinement, luxurious and highly sophisticated. As this neo-classical illustration demonstrates, the style displayed a great sense of proportion. Fabric was used to express and emphasize architectural qualities; here, to bring out the curve of an archway.*

Empire Style

left *Empire, a style associated with Napoleon, is a powerful look with strong colours and a certain masculinity. Again, there is a great sense of proportion and enough fabric is used to promote a sense of richness. Empire gains its masculinity from its association with imperial or war-like themes; brilliant colours are typical of the style.*

Biedermeier Interior

below *Biedermeier is an altogether different style, which arose in the comfortable middle-class homes of northern Europe at the beginning of the nineteenth century. This look was essentially devised by and for ordinary people, and the effect is bold and strong. What I find so appealing in this example is the marvellous use of colour and the confident stripe – not a hesitant or self-conscious look at all.*

Finishing Touches

above *Richness of detail, displayed in the finishing and trimming of fabric treatments, is particularly inspirational. Aside from the glorious combination of gilt and celadon, I am intrigued by the attention to detail in this picture, the fringing, tassels and edging which emphasizes the richness of the fabrics.*

Historical Notebook

Palladian Splendour

left *Malcontenta, the Palladian villa with its breathtaking frescoes by Veronese, is a favourite place. Visits there, and to other villas in the Brenta valley, were the inspiration for a recent collection which attempted to recapture some of the quality of fading frescoes as well as making use of traditional motifs from Italian fabrics.*

Simply Shaker

below *Early American styles, in particular the distinctive look which arose out of the Shaker movement in the eighteenth-nineteenth century, have a particular relevance for contemporary interiors. Although these rooms are austere and plain, they are never cold or uninviting. The use of clear colours and forthright geometrics is very appealing. The Shaker creed maintained very strict rules for the making and decoration of furniture; designs were spare, unelaborate and functional. To the modern eye, this distillation of form is beautiful and pure.*

Farmer's Rococo

left *Scandinavian styles of decoration have a similar appeal. Less rigorous than the Shaker interiors, rooms are nevertheless under-furnished and homely, and display a wonderful use of clear colours to make the most of natural light. The late eighteenth-century Lebell House in Kristinestad, Finland, is an example of 'farmer's rococo', an understated version of the grand French style. The flat check pelmet, which adds the finishing touch to the unlined white curtains, gives the interior a natural atmosphere rather than a pretentious look.*

Lace and Light

below *Light is a preoccupation in northern interiors. Here, lace is displayed flat against the windows making a delightful contrast with the lustrous painted floor and rough-cast wall. The dark wood of the window frames strengthens the look.*

Festoon Finery

above *This nineteenth-century Scandinavian interior is a perfect example of how to use festoon blinds – not in a nostalgic, overly romantic way. The contrast between the utility of the stove, the simplicity of the furnishings and decoration, and the prettiness of the festoon is very attractive.*

Pattern as a Focal Point

One of the simplest but most dramatic ways of using pattern is as a focus of attention. This strategy is one which is particularly effective in modern rooms.

Patterned fabric, with its strong traditional associations, fell out of fashion for a while among devotees of strict minimalist or high-tech monochrome interiors, but gradually people are beginning to see in what way fabric can be reintroduced into such contemporary schemes. Big, bright, abstract designs, large scale florals in rich colours and strong geometric prints are best: dainty rose chintz obviously does not go with the Bauhaus aesthetic.

Display the patterns in big blocks. You could add a black and white Roman blind to a monochrome dining room, for example, or cover sofas in a high-tech living room with a bright floral design. Even large floral table mats in a graphic-style dining room would be an effective, if simple, use of pattern: the witty clash of styles gives drama and life to the whole scheme.

Coordination

Twenty years ago there were no coordinated ranges of fabric on the market; today, coordination has become something of a safe option. It is now quite usual to see rooms decorated in a single design, perhaps with a matching plain fabric or with the same pattern reversed, or in a different size.

While this type of look has grown so popular as to be a little clichéd, coordination is nevertheless a very useful introduction to the notion of harmony in decoration. It teaches you to consider carefully all the elements in the room together, rather than approach them haphazardly and piecemeal. It is also a vivid demonstration of how scale and application can make a difference. The same pattern hanging in folds as curtains will look vastly different when placed flat on a small scale, as a cushion cover, or tailored, as upholstery.

The sheer impact of repeating a pattern over and over can be very dramatic and strong. Overall, however, I find a strict strategy of coordination rather limiting. I prefer to take the coordination up to a certain point and then inject a few discordant or clashing elements to give vitality to a scheme.

Mixing Patterns

For many people the art of mixing patterns has acquired something of a mystique, but, with practice it need not be prohibitively difficult and it is certainly one of the most rewarding ways of using pattern. In pattern-mixing it is not enough to coordinate colours or types of design: you have to look for some overall affinity and balance the composition in terms of scale and proportion.

Colour is a good place to begin. The patterns you choose should be linked colour-wise to one another. For example, one pattern may contain all the colours in the scheme, another pattern may just display one of those shades together with white, while another one may consist of two of the colours. In terms of design, as a general rule you cannot mix big patterns together that do not relate in some way. It is best to look for some type of affinity: for example, you can blend a floral chintz containing a stripe with another stripe and a small floral repeat. Finally, it is important to plan how these patterns will be applied, in other words to assess the proportion of each to the others. A large-scale pattern will affect the whole scheme much less radically if used as a trimming than if used as full-length curtains.

A useful tool in this process is the sample board. Sample boards are the means by which professional designers work out their ideas and then present them to their clients, but they consist of nothing more exotic than a large sheet of card to which samples of the materials selected have been attached and annotated. Your sample board can be put together in the same way, or it could be made up on a page in a scrapbook or on a kitchen noticeboard. See overleaf for sample boards.

Colour and Pattern Mixing

opposite A collection of cool blue fabrics used to upholster a sturdy period chair provides a touch of wit and an element of surprise in this simple interior. Colour is the element here that unifies the array of different-patterned fabrics. Another way to mix patterns while still creating a cohesive whole would be to use several different colours of the same pattern, held together with piped edges made in the same colour as each other.

When mixing patterns, always bear in mind what effect different pattern proportions have against one another. It is best to use large patterns only when you have a large area to fill, or alternatively, as a discreet piped or bound edging so that it does not detract from a more delicate pattern used over a smaller area.

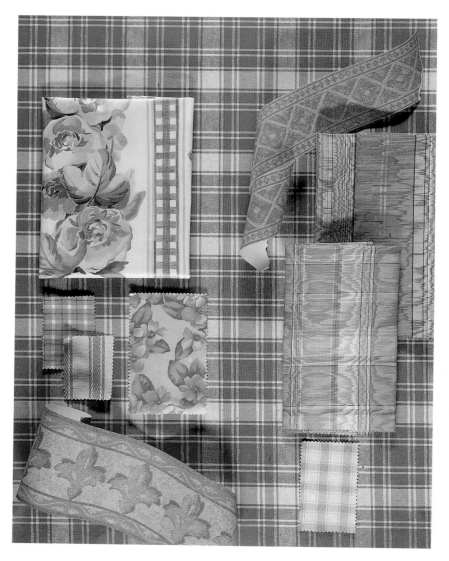

The essential reason for compiling a sample board is to provide yourself with a visual demonstration of the way in which all the fabric elements you intend to use will work together. This is especially useful if you are starting work from scratch. If, for example, you decide to completely revamp your living room by re-covering sofas and chairs, making new curtains and cushions and maybe painting walls at the same time, you will need to make a substantial outlay of money on new fabric. A sample board is absolutely necessary to give you an idea of the effect you want to achieve, especially if you decide to be a little more adventurous in your choice of fabric design and colour.

What you must not do is to collect only even-sized samples of each fabric or pattern and simply assemble them together in one place. Instead, you have to give yourself some idea of the proportion and application of each fabric.

If you are covering a sofa in one pattern and piping it in a sharp accent colour, then the sample of sofa fabric must be much bigger than the strip of accent piping. You can also try to fold or bunch fabric that will be draped, as with a generously gathered curtain for example, as opposed to those patterns which will be seen flat – on cushions or chairs. It will then be possible to see the pattern which your chosen fabrics will combine to produce, when used as soft furnishings. Remember it is much more economical of time and money to change your mind at this stage rather than later, when you have bought fabric and started to sew.

Creating Sample Boards

above and opposite *These two examples of sample boards show how useful it is to create an impression of the kind of fabrics you intend to use in an interior before final selection.*

Windows admit light and air, express the architectural qualities of a room by virtue of their detail and proportion and allow views of the outside world.

Despite their decorative importance, windows are often underestimated, their true potential neglected, with many window treatments being ill-conceived or off-the-peg solutions that are neither inspiring nor appropriate. This is a real pity, because with a little imagination window treatments can transform a room, maximizing the effect of natural light and lifting the decoration out of the ordinary.

Window treatments go far beyond the scope of simple department-store curtains or blinds. There are an immense number of variations on the theme, from gloriously swagged draperies, intricately trimmed, to charming effects with lengths of rich fabric requiring little or no sewing at all.

Windows

Setting the Style

Because it will have such an impact on the rest of the room, a window treatment cannot be chosen in isolation: it must be treated as an integral part of a decorative scheme. In practice, this means more than simple colour coordination or pattern matching, it means choosing a fabric and a treatment which will express a particular style. At the same time, how you dress a window must also suit its location, shape and size.

Period or traditional rooms often seem to call for full-length curtains with an appropriate pelmet and tie-backs. You can achieve a high degree of historical accuracy with the shape of the pelmet and style of trimmings. A special note of luxury can be introduced by fitting the curtains with contrasting linings or adding separate lightweight under-curtains. But this is not the only solution for traditional rooms. Georgian-style festoons in rich sateen would complement the classical elegance of eighteenth-century furnishings; tailored Roman blinds in a traditional print would not be out of place in a room which was less specific in its historical references.

On the other hand, contemporary rooms are often equipped with the more severe styles of window treatment – roller or Roman blinds in strong geometric patterns or solid bright colours are very typical of modern rooms. But it can be equally effective to play up the contrast with the hard-edged furniture and functional surfaces by covering windows with evocative drifts of plain muslin or with clever swathes of asymmetric drapery.

Window treatments are probably the single most important use of fabric in the home, and can represent a considerable investment. Before you commit yourself to a choice of fabric and a style, study the window itself. Is it wide or narrow, is it set high up or does it extend from floor to ceiling? Are the views worth looking at? Are there fine intrinsic features, such as stained glass, elegant glazing bars, arched tops? The way fabric is used can emphasize the good features of the window and its location and go some way towards remedy-ing its drawbacks. Full, gathered curtains extending out to either side of a narrow window will make it seem wider; a deep pelmet attached above a window head will lengthen a short window. If a view, window glass or window design is very beautiful, the fabric should be used as a frame for the whole picture, making a harmonious composition.

Finally, do not neglect the practical con-siderations. In these days of central heating, curtains are not as important as insulators as they once were, but they can still go a long way towards excluding draughts and reducing fuel bills. Window treatments are generally required to provide some degree of privacy; how much will depend on the room and your own preference. A total blackout of light can be achieved by lining curtains or blinds in the special fabric designed for the purpose.

Headings

The style of a curtain (or a gathered blind) will depend to a large extent on its heading, the means by which a fabric is gathered up and attached to a track or pole. The heading, usually achieved nowadays by attaching special heading tape to the curtain rather than by laborious hand sewing, will determine whether the curtain is formal with full folds, crisply pleated, softly gathered, shirred and so on.

Some headings look better on display, whereas others really should be covered by pelmets. Certain headings also suit particular types of fabric. Shirred or cased headings work best with lightweight fabrics such as muslin or lace; the more tailored, pleated headings suit crisp chintzes and heavier materials such as wools, brocades and damasks. Try to avoid pinch pleats which can look rather ordinary. Gathered heading styles are more natural and give a flowing, abundant look to soft, floral designs. Ties, bows, loops and other imaginative headings make a feature out of the means of suspension and they often work best in conjunction with quite plain fabrics such as unpatterned cotton.

Window Treatments

opposite Curtains made with generous swathes of fabric always look more appealing than skimpy rectangles of material stretched across a window. An interesting way of enriching the decorative effect of curtains is to line them with a contrasting fabric. Headings can be varied to create different effects; here a ruffled edge is embellished with fabric ties that fix the curtain to its track.

Look at window treatments in magazines or books, and learn to recognise what sort of treatments suit which kind of windows. Grand curtains fashioned from brocade and sporting elegant pelmets and lavish tie-backs would obviously look out of place in a modest country cottage. Similarly, simple rustic tie-on curtains would not fit well into a lavish period interior.

The width of material is an important consideration. Most heading tapes specify a required width: from one and a half to two and a half times the length of tape is usual. Err on the generous side as skimpy curtains are horrid.

Linings

The most interesting aspect of many window treatments is the effect they have on light. Light shining through an open-weave fabric such as lace creates dappled, romantic shadows; through a fine patterned fabric, light will be tinted. If privacy or warmth is not an issue, it can be highly effective to leave curtains or blinds unlined.

Lining, however, has many practical advantages. It prolongs the life of most curtains (as well as Roman and festoon blinds), increases insulation and provides a greater degree of privacy. A lined curtain also looks more professional and keeps its shape for longer. Interlining, which consists of adding a layer of 'bump' or blanketing material between curtain and lining, gives a curtain a full, rounded shape and blocks light and noise very effectively. But interlining can also have a deadening stuffy look and a simple lining is often more sympathetic.

Lining fabric need not be plain white or cream. You can choose a colour to act as a

Combination Curtains

An informal tie-blind which falls in gentle folds combines well with a simple curtain in a toning fabric. This effect is simple to achieve and works particularly well on long, narrow windows where you may want to pull a blind down during the day.

Bound-edged Fullness

Bound edges in a colour that features in the main fabric of a curtain add a neat finishing touch and in this instance also form an integral heading. These curtains are gathered in wide folds which provide fullness and enhance the way the pattern of the fabric is displayed.

Asymmetric Pelmet

A quick and easy way of creating this charming, informal pelmet is to gather a generous piece of fabric into neat folds and sew it together to form a full, draped pelmet. It can then be attached to your curtain track with either Velcro strips or fabric ties.

tinted background where the light shines through the main curtain fabric; or choose a contrasting pattern to display where the curtain edges are caught back.

Accessories and trimmings

Detail makes all the difference. It is always worth making the extra effort to add an edging, a fringe or a pelmet wherever these would be effective. In the past window treatments were enriched by a variety of trimmings, such as gold cord, fringing, tassels, bows and rosettes. Taste is rather more austere today but decorative details can still be enjoyable.

Included among details that are purely decorative are simple piped or banded edges, ribbon and braid. These supply a jolt of contrast, either of colour or texture, and can all be in a sharp accent colour because they are on such a small scale. Braid, gimp, fringing and tassels add textural interest and movement. Ties, bows and frills emphasize fullness.

Accessories such as pelmets and tie-backs make important finishing touches. There are many shapes and styles to coordinate with the fabric and style treatment you have chosen. Pelmets can be flat and shaped, pleated, gathered or box, or full draped swags while tie-backs range from heavy tasselled cord to shaped holdbacks.

Sloping Blinds

For attic rooms, these blinds offer a neat way of keeping out light. They are held in place by means of cords placed either side of the blind. The cords run through screw eyes which have been attached to stiffened fabric bands that run across the back of the blind at regular intervals.

Rustic Charm

These simple edged curtains provide a charming frame for two very small and traditional windows. Made with rich, heavy fabric, they hang in a neat, formal manner that exactly matches the style of the furniture in the room.

Wall-to-wall Curtains

When using curtains to cover not only a large window, but also the space either side of it, take full advantage of having a big space to play with and choose a fabric that incorporates a bold, dramatic pattern repeat.

Tie-on Curtains

Either sill-length or down to the floor, these tie-on curtains make a pretty alternative to more conventionally headed versions. The crisp side edging is achieved by bringing a margin of the lining around to the front. A contrasting colour or pattern is a good choice for lining fabric; ties can match this material and are simply looped onto rings and tied into bows. You can buy lengths of tape or ribbon or make the ties from fabric.

Materials

Main fabric
Contrasting fabric for lining and ties, if desired
Tape or ribbon for ties, if desired
Heading tape

Measuring up

For the width of each curtain you will need to measure the pole and multiply measurement x required fullness (in this case, one and a half times the width) and halve. For each curtain, cut the main fabric to these measurements and the lining fabric 6cm (2¼in) wider than these measurements. Cut each piece to the desired finished length. Also cut two strips from the contrasting fabric, each the finished width of the curtain, adding 2.5cm (1in) for turning in the ends, and 6cm (2¼in) wide. For each tie you will need two strips of contrasting fabric, each measuring 5 x 22cm (2 x 9in).
You will also need a strip of interfacing for each curtain measuring the finished width of the curtain and 10cm (4in) deep.

Making up

1 Position the heading tape 1.5cm (⅝in) down from top edge of wrong side of the main fabric and press.

2 Lay the main fabric on the lining, right sides together, aligning side edges and sew 1.5cm (⅝in) seams. Press seams open.

3 Turn curtain right side out and adjust so that an equal amount of lining shows each side when main fabric is facing and press.

4 Fold 1.5cm (⅝in) to wrong side along each side of the edging strips and press. Bring folded edges together and press again.

5 Lay the edging strips along top and bottom edges of main fabric side of the curtain, right sides together, aligning raw edges, leaving 1.2cm (½in) overlaps at each end. Sew 1.5cm (⅝in) seams through all layers. Bring edging up over seams to lining side of the curtain, turning overlaps at ends over bound edges, and slip-stitch into place covering the machine stitching.

6 Pin heading tape to top of curtain 3.5cm (1½in) from top edge. Stitch and gather up.

7 Make the ties by folding each strip in half down its length, right sides together, and sewing a 1cm (⅜in) seam down the side and across one end. Trim seam, clip corner, turn right side out and press. Attach ties in pairs to top of heading tape, spacing them evenly and turning raw edges.

Lined Curtains

Lined curtains not only hang better and last longer, they offer more decorative possibilities too. Choose a lining that complements or contrasts with the main fabric and display it by hooking back the leading edges of the curtains with tie-backs. For a professional finish with conventional or decorative linings, lock stitch the lining in place as directed here.

These curtains are headed with a simple gathered tape which leaves a stand-up frill. You can allow the curtains to drape onto the floor for additional richness or trim the inner edges with fringe, braid or gimp *(see page 120)*.

Materials

Main fabric
Contrasting fabric
Iron-on heavyweight interfacing
Heading tape
Long ruler
Curtain hooks
Pencil

Measuring up

Measure the desired length and width of one curtain. Add 15cm (6in) to the length for heading and hem. For each curtain measure the width of the track or pole and multiply measurement x required fullness, (in this case one and a half times the width) and halve if you have to join widths of fabric, join flat seams and press open; if using patterned fabric, allow for an extra pattern repeat when measuring up. For the lining you will need the same amount of fabric per curtain less 13cm (5in) on the width and 15cm (6in) on the length (i.e., the same length as the finished curtain). You will also need two strips of iron-on interfacing, each measuring the finished width of the curtain and 5cm (2in) deep.

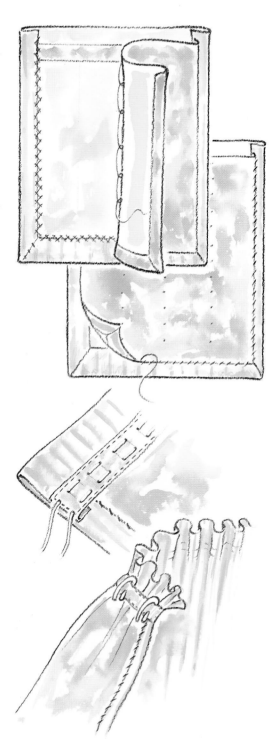

Making up

1 Press each strip of interfacing to wrong side of main fabric 5cm (2in) from top edge and same amount in from each side edge.

2 Turn 5cm (2in) in to wrong side down each side and 10cm (4in) up along bottom and press. Mitre the corners *(see page 58)* and herringbone or slip-stitch into place.

3 Draw vertical lines down whole length of curtain on reverse side, using the long ruler and pencil, 30cm (12in) apart, starting in the centre.

4 Turn 2cm (¾in) in to wrong side down each side of lining and 5cm (2in) up along bottom and press. Mitre the corners and stitch as main fabric.

5 Place the lining on the main fabric, wrong sides together, matching hems and sides so top of lining sits 5cm (2in) down from top of main fabric, and pin lining to main fabric down centre.

6 Working from the centre out, fold lining back so it lies perfectly flat along pencil lines on reverse of main fabric, sewing long, loose locking stitches *(see page 117)* down each line, picking up only one or two threads of main fabric, spacing each stitch about 10cm (4in) from the previous one, doing this along each line in turn.

7 Slip-stitch lining to side and bottom hems of main fabric.

8 Turn top edge of main fabric in to lining side along top edge of lining and cover raw edge with the tape, leaving 3.5cm (1½in) for the stand-up frill. Turn under the ends, knot cords at the ends that will be the inner edges and machine stitch along sides and ends of tape, leaving cords free for gathering, and sewing along each side in same direction to avoid puckering or twisting material.

9 Pull the cords to gather the curtains to the right width and tie off. Attach hooks and hang the curtains.

D r e s s   C u r t a i n s

These shaped curtains make a flattering frame for a small window. They are caught back to display the contrasting lining fabric, a treatment which further emphasizes their long curved inner edges. The draped pelmet is also lined so that it hangs well.

Both curtains and pelmet are fixed in position. 'Dress' curtains – those which are not intended to draw – can be combined with inner draw curtains or blinds if privacy is required.

Materials

Main fabric
Two contrasting fabrics for lining and binding
  (see page 120)
Lining for pelmet
Heading tape or ties
Paper
Pencil

Measuring up

For the curtains you will need to measure the width of the window, halving this amount for each curtain (add a little extra if more fullness is required), and from the top of the track or the bottom edge of the rings to the desired length. You will also need an equal amount of contrasting fabric for the lining adding 1.5cm (⅝in) all round for seam allowances. For the pelmet you will need to measure the length of the track or pole and add half again. For the depth of the pelmet, decide how far down the window you want the finished pelmet to hang, adding 1.5cm (⅝in) all round for seam allowances. Remember to allow for extra fabric at the top, depending on your method of hanging.

You will also need enough fabric to make sufficient 6cm-(2⅜in-) wide binding to bind the straight and curved edges of the curtains, adding 2.5cm (1in) for turning in the ends. Allow enough fabric for ties if required *(see page 42).*

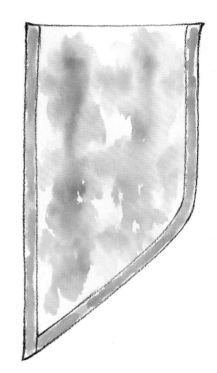

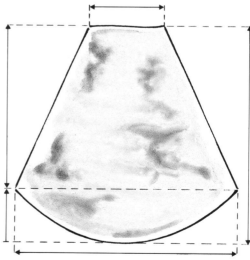

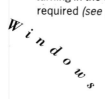

Making up

1 Make a curtain pattern. Cut a piece of paper to curtain measurements, marking sill level on right-hand vertical edge. Draw a gentle curve from this point into bottom left-hand corner. Cut out your pattern.

2 Measure and cut a rectangular pattern for the pelmet, measuring 1½ times the finished width by 2½ times the required finished drop. Draw and cut out the pattern shape from the diagram.

3 Using the pattern, cut out two curtains pieces from each of the main and lining fabrics. Cut out the valance – one piece from main fabric, one from lining.

4 With wrong side facing, tack curtain and lining pieces together. Turn 1.5cm (⅝in) to wrong side along top. Finish with ties *(see page 42)* or heading tape *(see page 36).*

5 Bind curved, then straight edges of curtains *(see page 120).* Press bound edges and hang curtains.

6 Attach a ring to the back of each curtain and fix a metal screw cup to the wall at sill level.

7 To make the valance, lay the two pieces of fabric wrong sides together, pin and sew 1.5cm (⅝in) seam along the curved edge. Turn right side out and press.

8 Pleat top of valance as shown, until overall width just overlaps ends of pole or track. Machine a 1.5cm (⅝in) seam to secure.

9 Fix a batten to the wall above the window and staple or tack the valance to it.

Curtain   Accessories

Accessories such as tie-backs complete a window treatment, adding decorative detail and a professional finish. The tie-back, of course, has a practical use too, keeping curtains neat and secure when open. The style of the tie-back and its trimming can complement the overall character of the window treatment; the position of the tie-back — at midpoint, above or below — determines the silhouette of the curtains.

Bound-edge tie-backs

Materials

Main fabric
Lightweight iron-on interfacing
Contrasting fabric or purchased binding for edging
Hook and curtain ring or bracket
Paper
Pencil

Measuring up

Work out the length you want the tie-back to be by draping a tape measure loosely around the curtain at the desired height, adding sufficient to tie and hang down, then decide on the width (remembering that if it is too wide it will be difficult to tie). You will need enough of the main fabric to accommodate two of these shapes for each tie-back.
You will need enough interfacing to accommodate one of the shapes for each tie-back.
You will also need enough contrasting fabric to make four binding strips *(see page 120)* 6cm (2¼in) wide, two the same length as the long sides of the tie-back and two the length of the ends, adding 2cm (¾in) to each for turning under, or this amount of purchased binding.

Curtain Tie-backs

Tie-backs offer a neat and luxurious finishing touch to generous curtains.
above *A bound-edge tie-back echoes the bound edges of the curtain and provides a crisp, defining line.*
left *Fringing is used here in complementary colours and in red to break up the blue and green of the curtains.*

Piped-edge tie-backs

Materials

Main fabric
Heavyweight iron-on interfacing
Piping purchased or handmade *(see page 121)*
Paper
Saucer
Pencil
Hook
Two curtain rings

Measuring up

Loosely loop a tape measure around the curtain at the desired height, holding the ends where the finished tie-back will hook to the wall. This gives you the length of the tie-back. Then decide how wide you want it to be. You will need enough main fabric to accommodate these dimensions twice for each tie-back plus 4cm (1½in) for seam allowances.
You will need enough interfacing to accommodate one of these dimensions.
You will also need enough piping to go round the edge of the tie-back, adding 4cm (1½in) for overlapping the ends.

Making the Patterns

Make a paper pattern by drawing a rectangle the finished width of the tie-back and half the finished length. The bound-edge tie-back has one vertical end and one slightly sloped end. The piped-edge tie-back has rounded ends which can be drawn around a saucer.

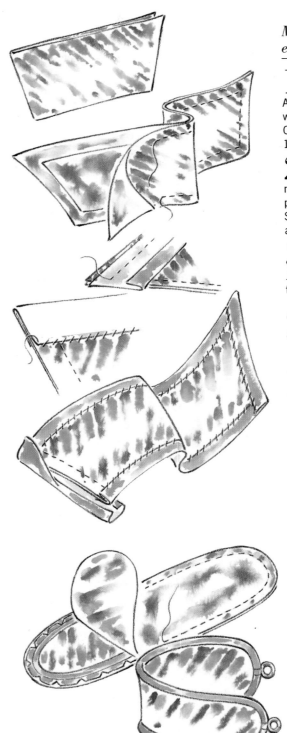

Making up bound-edge tie-backs

1 Fold main fabric in half, selvedge to selvedge. Align vertical edge of pattern with fold, cut out two pieces. Cut out interfacing, trim off 1.5cm (⅝in) all round.

2 Iron interfacing centrally on wrong side of one of main fabric pieces. Place fabric pieces wrong sides together. Sew 1cm (⅜in) seam all around.

3 Prepare and attach binding strips *(see page 120)*, first to long edges, then to short, turning in overlaps.

4 To attach tie-back to wall by hook, sew curtain ring at centre of right side.

Making up piped-edge tie-backs

1 Fold fabric in half, selvedge to selvedge. Aligning straight end of pattern with fold, cut out two pieces, adding 1.5cm (⅝in) seam allowances. Cut out interfacing, without seam allowance. Iron interfacing on wrong side of one of fabric pieces.

2 Make up and insert piping *(see page 121)*. Turn tie-back out. Slip-stitch closed.

3 Sew a curtain ring to each end of tie-back. Fix the hook to the wall.

Simple Tie Blind

In certain situations, particularly where a view is less than marvellous or privacy is important, it may be desirable to screen a window at least partially all the time. Ideal for such a purpose is this simple unlined blind, which allows light through but blocks unwelcome sights. The blind is held up with strips of tape or ribbon attached to the top and tied in place at the bottom edge. It is not designed to be raised or lowered frequently.

Only lightweight fabrics are really suitable, but they can be teamed with heavier outer curtains or lined curtains made with the same fabric. The blind can be fixed directly to the top of the window frame with Velcro or, if you want it to hang away from the glass, on a batten screwed to the wall or window frame.

Materials

Main fabric
Ties, made of the same fabric, contrasting tape or
    narrow ribbon
Batten, painted to match wall or window frame, if
    desired, and screws
Velcro, sew- or iron-on type

Measuring up

You will need a piece of fabric measuring the width of the window, adding 5cm (2in) for hems, and measuring the desired final length, adding enough for a small fold when tied and 5cm (2in) for heading and hem (allow a little more if fitting to a batten). You will also need four equal lengths of tape, ribbon or fabric to make ties measuring length of blind plus sufficient to tie into bows. For fabric ties, cut four strips, each 5cm (2in) wide.

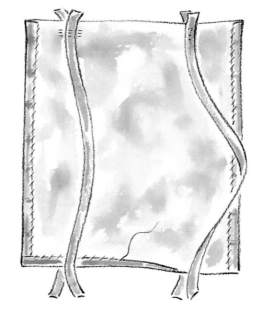

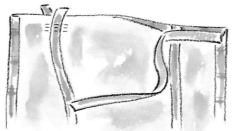

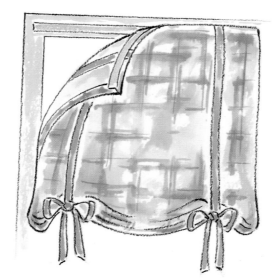

Making up

1 Turn under 1.2cm (½in) to wrong side, turn under same again and stitch into place carefully.

2 If making ties of fabric, turn in 1cm (⅜in) to the long wrong side, down the long edges. Bring long folded edges together and machine stitch close to edges down lengths and across ends.

3 Stitch ties to top of blind at same point front and back, about a quarter of the width of the blind in from each side, securing with several rows of stitching.

4 Turn heading allowance in to wrong side, turning corners in neatly. Lay soft half of Velcro over raw edge and sew or iron into place.

5 Stick or tack other half of Velcro to the top edge of the batten and then press blind into place.

6 Roll up blind to required height and tie the ties in neat bows.

R o m a n   B l i n d

Roman blinds are tailored without being stark, soft without being fussy, making a perfect complement to drawn curtains as well as an elegant feature in their own right. They often look particularly handsome when finished with a bound edge which accentuates the neat folds of fabric.

Roman blinds are usually made of good-quality curtain material and lined in cotton sateen. Avoid large round designs that look odd when pulled up. Stripes are crisp and fresh, but a severely rectilinear pattern may pull out of alignment and make the blind look crooked and badly made.

Roman blinds are easy to make but accuracy when measuring, marking and sewing is essential. The folds are formed by lengths of dowel in carriers attached to the back and hooked up with rings and cords. The blind is then stapled or tacked to a batten which is then screwed to the wall or window frame. To hang the blind inside a window reveal, attach the batten to the underside of the reveal. To hang outside the reveal, paint the batten the colour of the wall or cover it with a matching fabric, as it will remain visible. If there already is a curtain track, attach curtain heading tape to the top of the blind, leaving the tape

Making up

1 Lay main fabric on the lining, wrong sides together, aligning edges and corners and checking that it lies perfectly flat. Sew 1cm (⅜in) seam down sides and along bottom edge.

2 On each edging strip fold in edges by 1.5cm (⅝in) and press. Bring folded edges together and press again. Open out. Pin the two long edging strips to the side edges of the right side of the blind, right sides together, and sew 1.5cm (⅝in) seams. Lift edging up over seam allowance to lining side, turn under pressed fold and slip-stitch neatly into place, covering line of stitching. Pin last strip to bottom edge of blind, leaving equal overlaps at each end and sew seam. Fold overlaps over bound side edges to wrong side, fold binding over seam allowance to wrong side and slip-stitch as sides, including ends.

3 Lay blind flat, wrong side up, bottom edge nearest you, and pin layers together at the top. Draw a horizontal line from side edge to side edge 6cm (2½in) down from top edge. Check that the line is at right angles to the sides using the set square. This will be the line for the batten.

4 Adjusting the spacing to have equal gaps between each carrier, draw placement lines for the carriers about 25 to 30cm (10 to 12in) apart. The lowest line should be a little over half this measurement up from the bottom edge, above the edging so it can be seen when the blind is drawn up.

ungathered, and use curtain hooks to suspend the blind from the ceiling.

This blind is lined, with a bound edge, but the lining can be turned over the main fabric for an edging. For a blind without edging, the main fabric must be cut wider than the lining so the seams appear at the back.

Materials

Main fabric
Lining
Contrasting fabric for edging (optional)
Pencil
Long ruler and set square
1.2cm (½in) dowels, cut to finished width less 2cm (¾in)
5 x 2.5cm (2 x 1in) batten, cut to finished width of blind
2.5cm (1in) wide lath
Cord
Rings
Two screw eyes
Stapling gun or tacks and hammer
Cleat

Measuring up

You will need a rectangle of the main fabric cut to the finished width of the blind, adding 3cm (1¼in) for seam allowances if unbound, and finished length of the blind, adding 6cm (2¼in) for the heading.

You will need a rectangle of lining fabric cut to the same measurements as the main fabric, plus the required number of strips for carriers, each measuring width of blind in length, adding 2.5cm (1in) for neatening ends, and 8cm (3¼in) wide.

You will also need three lengths of edging 6cm (2½in) wide: two measuring the length of the blind, one the width of the blind, adding 2.5cm (1in) for neatening ends (see page 120 for making up edging).

You will need to cut two lengths of cord that are twice the length of the blind, plus its width.

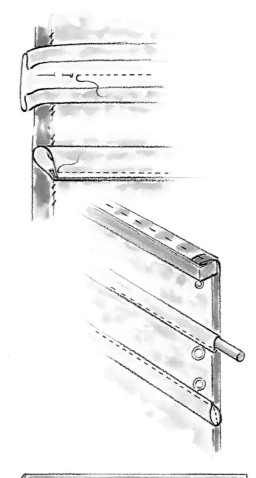

5 To make the carriers, turn in and press 1cm (⅜in) along the edges of the lining strips. Bring the pressed edges together and press so that there is a centre crease. Lay carrier strips wrong side up on lining of blind with centre creases along placement lines with a 1.2cm (½in) allowance overhanging at each end (first line is for batten). Stitch along creases using matching thread to main fabric. Turn in the overlaps, bring the folded edges together and stitch close to the edge, leaving the ends open. Stitch rings at each end exactly in line vertically.

6 Drill holes in batten where you want to screw it to the wall. Turn in the top edge of the blind 2cm (¾in) and press. Lay the batten on the wrong side of the blind, aligning its top front edge with the top placement line. Bring the fabric over the top and staple to the batten.

7 Fix screw eyes to underside of the batten in line with the rings. Insert the dowel in the carriers and the lath in the bottom and slip-stitch the ends closed.

8 Tie a length of cord to each of the bottom rings, thread it up through the rings and screw eyes and take one cord across to the pulling side. Knot the cords at the top, just outside the edge of the blind. Trim ends and knot again.

9 Screw the batten to the wall, holding the fabric clear. Fix the cleat to the wall.

Festoon Blind

The festoon blind combines the fullness of a curtain with the operation of a blind. Pulled up by means of cords and rings like a Roman blind, it is headed by tape and hooked onto a track like a curtain. Special vertical tapes, which gather the fabric as well as providing loops for the cords, enable the ruched effect to be maintained when the blind is lowered.

Festoons originated at the beginning of the eighteenth century when they consisted of billowing hangings drawn up to the top of the window adding elegance and drama to the sparsely furnished Georgian interior. To emulate this period look, the blind can be made in sumptuous fabric, as long as the material is light enough to draw up easily. Festoons may also be lined. This unlined example exploits the effect of light filtering through it and is decorated with braid over the tape lines and fringing at the bottom. Festoons lend themselves to trimming – with frills, bows and rosettes being particularly popular.

Festoons are generally corded at the edges. This example, with its trailing sides, omits the edge tapes – an effect which is only possible if you are using lightweight fabric.

Special festoon or Austrian blind tracks exist which have holes to take the pull-up cords. Alternatively, you can fix an ordinary curtain track onto a wooden batten, which is needed for fixing the screw eye to. If there is already a track at the window, the screw eye can be fixed into the window frame.

Materials

Main fabric
Festoon blind tape
Braid (optional)
Cord
Fringing
Curtain heading tape
Curtain track or special Austrian blind track
Curtain hooks
Large screw eye
Batten
Drill
Tacks and hammer
Cleat

Measuring up

Fullness of the blind will be dictated by the heading tape you use, so see the manufacturer's instructions. Standard tape usually requires one and a half times width of fabric to tape. Similarly, you will need one and a quarter times fabric to tape for the length. Add 4cm (1½in) to the width for the side hems and 6cm (2⅜in) to the length for the heading and hem. You will need enough lengths of festoon blind tape measuring length of the blind to enable finished blind to have gaps between tapes of about 30cm (12in) once heading tape has been gathered. You will need same amount of cord, adding sufficient to take across top of blind and down to cleat. You will also need the same amount of braid, if you are adding this decoration, and a length of fringing measuring the width of the blind, adding 1cm (⅜in) for neatening ends, if using.

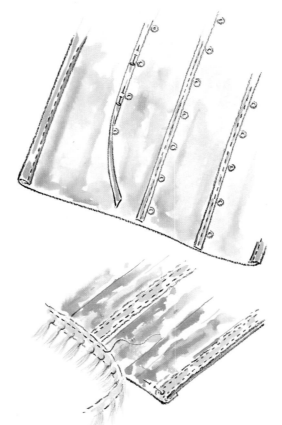

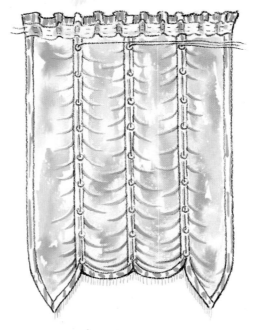

Making up

1 Mark positions of tapes, across the fabric – leaving equal-sized gaps, by folding and pressing blind vertically. If you need to join widths of fabric, make sure that join is covered by a line of tape. Turn 1cm (⅜in) in to wrong side down each side, turn in same again and machine stitch.

2 Cut the required number of lengths of festoon tape, pin to back of blind with centre of tape placed on fold lines and stitch down centre. Ensure that loops align horizontally and that first loop is 2.5cm (1in) from the bottom.

3 If desired, attach braid to the right side of the blind to cover the stitching of side seams and tape. Machine stitch both edges, taking care not to catch the sides of the tape.

4 Turn up a 1cm (⅜in) hem along bottom of blind, repeat, press and tack. Lay the fringing along the right side of the hem and stitch into place. At the top, turn down 4cm (1½in) and attach heading tape.

5 Pull the cords in the vertical tapes to gather the blind to the required drop and tie off. Gather the heading tape to the required width and tie off. Tie cords to bottom loops and thread through to the top.

6 Attach the blind to the curtain track with hooks and bring the cords across the top of the blind and thread them through the large screw eye on the pulling side. Fix cleat to wall.

Cushions are all about comfort. Piled on a sofa or scattered in deep armchairs, they immediately give a room an atmosphere which is both inviting and informal.

But they are also an enjoyable and flexible means of displaying fabric. Covers can be changed season by season without too much trouble or expense, providing an instant facelift or change of mood. You can experiment with unusual fabrics which are not traditionally used in soft furnishing, or display precious pieces of needlework or antique materials.

Most importantly, the choice of colours, textures and patterns can work to draw the whole decorative scheme together. Simple coordination, or repetition of patterns used for upholstery or curtains, is one option but it is more satisfying and effective to add a few surprises, injecting vitality into the overall scheme.

Cushions

Setting the Style

Defined Edges

above *Three rows of embroidery in different colours help to define coordinating cushions and upholstery.* opposite *A vivid yellow cushion is fringed in contrasting colours to those used on the curtains.*

Cushion Fabrics

Wherever you intend to place a cushion it is a good idea to choose the fabric for the cover in conjunction with its background – that is, the piece of furniture against which it will be displayed. Cushions are a particularly good way of visually breaking up the expanse of a sofa or bed, both of which might otherwise dominate a room. Obviously, the sofa upholstery or bedcover will have an important effect on your choice of cushion cover for these pieces of furniture.

With a little careful planning, the fabrics you display on cushions can tie together the entire decoration of a room, although strict coordination is a little dull. If you have six cushions on a sofa, they should not be all of the same fabric, or all trimmed in the same manner. But, on the other hand, they shouldn't be all different, either. Six different patterns, six different trimmings and six different shapes

would be visual chaos. Out of the six, plan for three to relate in some way, three to be different; perhaps two cushions might be identical to each other.

Repeating the same fabric that you have already used for curtains or seating is an obvious way of introducing harmony. But another more subtle strategy is to cover cushions in a fabric which you have already used as an accent – as a trimming or lining, for example – and trim the cushion in the main fabric. This type of witty reversal can add a tremendous sense of life to a room, with a large bold repeat, for example, used on a tiny scale as piping, supplying a hint of fabric coordination, rather than resorting to the predictable repetition of the same fabric for curtains or blinds, sofas, chairs and cushions.

Contrast and Accent

Cushions can be an important means of supplying contrast and accent – featuring bright, jolting colours or unusual textures. And they can make an amusing contrast of styles. Cushion covers are an excellent way of using fabric in a contemporary room. A large black-and-white floral print, checked or tapestry cushions would look simply stunning on a modern black leather sofa, while a combination of striped cushions against upholstery in a different stripe make for an interesting pattern mix.

The shape of a cushion and the style of its trimming are other considerations. Square or rectangular cushions are probably the most versatile and practical; 'novelty' shapes may be fun for a while but their appeal will soon fade. Bolster shapes are rather formal and suit some period styles of furnishing, particularly the classical lines of Empire and Regency. Trimmings such as piping, edging, flat embroidered borders and frills each add their own look, from tailored elegance to a softer, more feminine style.

Cushions 50

S q u a r e   C u s h i o n s

Cushions are one of the simplest fabric accessories to make and provide an instant splash of colour. Almost any fabric is suitable. As well as furnishing fabrics, you can experiment with dress materials, such as velvets, tweeds and lace (on fabric backing) or display a piece of needlework or kelim rug.

Square cushions are the most popular, versatile shape. Square pads come in different sizes, so choose the size to suit the piece of furniture. Square cushion covers are very easy to make. They can be fastened in a variety of ways, including zips, Velcro and sewing. Cushions with back vent openings should only be made in lightweight fabrics otherwise the closing becomes overly bulky.

The methods of closing cushions described on this page apply equally well to round and rectangular cushions.

Materials

Main fabric
Cushion pad
Press studs, Velcro spots, shirt buttons or zip, 7.5cm (3in) shorter than cushion side or width

Measuring up

You will need two squares of main fabric whose sides measure width of cushion pad from seam to seam across its centre, adding 3cm (1¼in) to each measurement for seam allowances (for a full, plump cushion, make the finished cover 2.5cm/1in smaller all round than pad). See different methods of closure below for measurement variations.

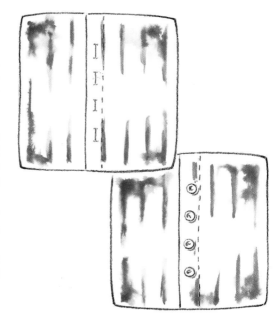

Making up

Button-back seam

1 Follow steps 1 & 2 of Back vent opening *(page 54)*.

2 Tack together hemmed edges and mark positions of buttonholes and buttons. Remove tacking and work button holes, either by hand or by machine.

3 Finish as step 3 on page 54 but sew on buttons before pressing.

Press studs or Velcro spots

1 Cut two squares of fabric as before (including seam allowances) but adding 3cm (1¼in) to depth of each square. Turn under 1.5cm (⅝in) to wrong side along one of shorter edges of each square, turn under same again and sew into place.

2 With right sides together, sew 5cm (2in) long seams in from each side just beneath hem, leaving a central opening.

3 Stitch press studs or Velcro spots to the right side of the opening edges along hem.

4 With right sides together, sew 1.5cm (⅝in) seams around the remaining three sides, sewing over the sides of the hems. Trim seams, clip corners, turn right side out and press.

Z i p s   a n d   V e n t s

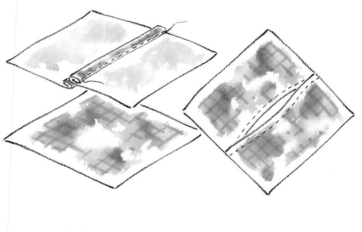

Back vent opening

1 Cut one square of fabric as before (including seam allowances) but for second square, add a further 11cm (4½in) to the depth then cut in half across depth of square.

2 Turn under 1.5cm (⅝in) to wrong side along long edges of second square (i.e. each side of the horizontal cut), turn under same again and machine or hand sew hems. Then, overlap hemmed edges by 5cm (2in).

3 Lay front on back piece, right sides together, and sew 1.5cm (⅝in) seam all round. Trim seams, clip corners, turn right side out and press.

4 Slip-stitch vent down 5cm (2in) in from each end.

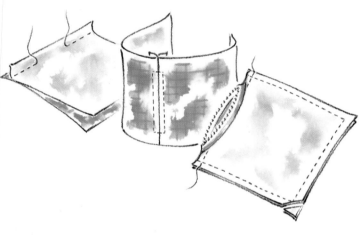

Zip in seam

1 Cut out two squares of fabric as before (including seam allowances), lay them right sides together, matching edges and corners, and sew 5cm (2in) long flat seams 1.5cm (⅝in) in from each end, leaving an opening for zip. Tack opening along seam line.

2 Press seam open, lay zip wrong side up along tacked part of seam and sew neatly into place from right side (see page 119). Undo tacking and open zip.

3 Lay back on front, right sides together, matching edges and corners, and sew 1.5cm (⅝in) seam round remaining three sides. Trim seams, clip corners, turn right side out and press.

Zip across back

1 Cut one square as before, (including seam allowances), but for second square, add a further 3cm (1¼in) to depth, then cut in half across depth of square.

2 Align two pieces of second square along halfway cut, right sides together, and sew 5cm (2in) long 1.5cm (⅝in) seams in from each end, leaving an opening for the zip in the middle. Tack opening along seam line.

3 Press seam open, lay zip wrong side up along tacked part of seam and sew neatly into place from the right side (see page 119). Undo tacking and open zip.

4 Lay back on front, right sides together, matching edges and corners, and sew 1.5cm (⅝in) seam all round. Trim seams, clip corners, turn right side out and press.

Round Cushions

Materials

As Square Cushions (*see page 53*) plus a sheet of tissue, greaseproof, brown or other similar large sheet of flexible paper, pencil, string and drawing pin. If using a zip, it should be 10cm (4in) shorter than diameter of cushion.

Measuring up

Measure cushion pad across its centre and add 3cm (1¼in) to this sum for seam allowances. (For a full, plump cushion, make finished cover 5cm/2in smaller in diameter than cushion pad.)

Making a pattern

To ensure that the fabric is perfectly circular, you must make a paper pattern. Cut out a square from the paper, making the sides the diameter of the pad, plus the seam allowances. Fold the square into quarters and then mark the perimeter by inserting a drawing pin at the folded corner (have a cork coaster or piece of cardboard underneath it to protect your table) and tie a piece of string to the drawing pin at one end and to the pencil at the other, making the distance between them the length of one of the sides. Use the string like a compass to trace the quadrant, cut along the line you have made and then unfold your pattern.

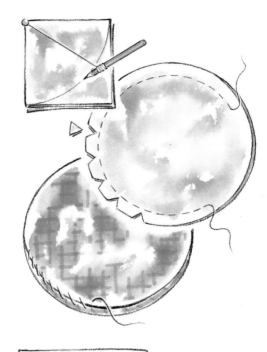

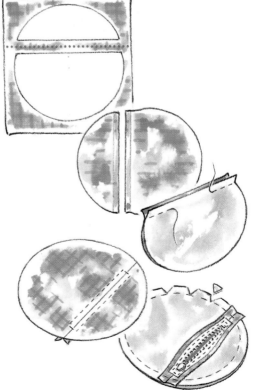

Making up

Slip-stitched seam

1 Use the pattern to cut out two pieces of fabric.

2 Lay the circles one on top of the other, right sides together, and sew a 1.5cm (⅝in) seam, leaving an opening large enough for the pad.

3 Notch seam allowance and turn right side out.

4 Press seam, insert pad and slip-stitch opening.

Zip across back

1 Cut across the pattern one third of the way down. Lay the two pieces on the fabric, leaving 3cm (1¼in) gap for seam allowances for the zip. Draw a line along the centre of the gap.

2 Cut round the pattern and along the line.

3 Align the two halves of back of cushion along zip seam, right sides together, and sew 5cm (2in) long 1.5cm (⅝in) seams at each end. Tack opening along seam line.

4 Press seam open, lay zip wrong side up along tacked part of seam and sew in place (*see page 119*). Undo tacking and open zip.

5 Lay back on front, right sides together, and sew 1.5cm (⅝in) seam all round.

6 Notch into seam allowance, turn right side out and press.

Piping

Piping

Piping gives a neat, crisp edge which outlines the cushion shape and gives it a finished appearance. Piping can be in the same fabric as the cushion cover or in a coordinating plain shade if the main fabric is patterned, but it can be very exciting to opt for a bright contrast to add a sharp graphic sense. A rather witty treatment for a plain cushion is to make piping from a patterned fabric, matching a curtain fabric, for example. The slice of pattern visible in the piping coordinates subtly.

You can buy piping from furnishing departments or make it yourself (*see page 121*). It consists of a long strip of bias-cut fabric, either folded or filled with cord, and inserted into the seams of upholstery or covers. It is available in various thicknesses, with thicker varieties commonest in soft furnishing.

Measuring up

Measure all the edges to be piped and cut a continuous strip of piping to match. If necessary to join two pieces of piping, add an extra 5cm (2in) for each join. See piping techniques, page 121.

Materials

Fabric for cushion cover with side openings for zip *(see page 54)*
Piping, purchased or made yourself *(see page 121)*
Zip

Making up

1 Lay piping along edges of right side of front piece of cushion cover with rounded edge inside of seam line and tack into place, clipping into the piping seam allowance at the corners. Join the end of piping in the centre of one side, either butting the cord together or unravelling the threads and twisting them together, folding under piping fabric and overlapping other end to neaten. For round cushions, snip notches into the seam allowance all round *(see page 118)*.

2 Lay front on back cover, right sides together, and sew 5cm (2in) long 1.5cm (⅝in) seams in from each end. Tack the opening along seam line.

3 Open seam on wrong side and press seam allowance of back of cover back on itself. Open zip, lay one half right side down with teeth against the piping and stitch in place to the front seam allowance.

4 Turn cover to right side, open out flat, close zip, and stitch along the unsewn edge of zip and across ends, checking that seam allowance is still folded back.

5 Fold cover right sides together, carefully align edges and corners and sew 1.5cm (⅝in) seam around remaining sides. Undo tacking, trim seams, clip corners, turn right side out and press.

Trimming

Cushions lend themselves to additional embellishment in the form of edging, borders, embroidery, frills and piping – all of which contribute neatness of finish and additional decorative interest. As well as these trimmings, which you can make yourself, there is a wide variety of ready-made decorative edgings, cords and fringes which can be bought and applied. Many of these have a traditional quality and would work well in a period room.

Flat borders

Materials

Main fabric
Cushion pad
Toning or contrasting thread for embroidered borders
Zip

Measuring up

As for the Square cushion cover *(see page 53)*, adding extra for required depth of border.
For Embroidered flat border, add an extra 2cm (¾in) to required depth of border.
For Flat double border, add double the required depth of border and seam allowance of 1.5cm (⅝in).

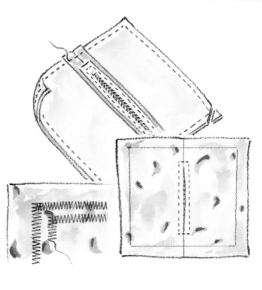

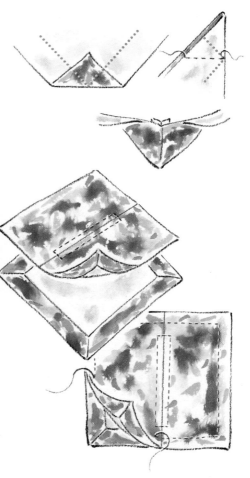

Making up

Embroidered flat border

1 Make cushion cover as cover with zip across back *(see page 55)*, when pressing make sure seam runs exactly along edge.

2 Measure in from the edge the required depth of the border along each side and draw a square on the fabric.

3 Tack along the line, then machine satin stitch using contrasting colour if desired. (Start the stitching halfway along the edge to avoid pulling the corners.) Sew a second line of satin stitch 1.2cm (½in) outside the first.

Flat double border

1 Make back section as for cover with zip across back *(see page 55)*.

2 Fold borders to inside and press. Open out border and, with wrong side facing, fold each corner to inside to form diagonal and press.

3 Open out again and bring outer edges of corner together, right sides facing, and sew along diagonal. Repeat for all other corners, trim seams and press open.

4 Turn wrong side of corner seams to inside and press the now mitred corners again.

5 On right side, measure in from the edge the required depth of the border along each side and draw a square on the fabric.

6 Lay the front of the cushion on the back, wrong sides together, and stitch along pencil lines.

Frills

Frills added to a cushion provide a feminine finish and a decorative effect. You can add frills to cushions that are made from the same fabric as the cover, in a contrasting fabric or in both. Frills can be trimmed with binding, piping or pinking. Double frills – made with a double thickness of fabric – are particularly luxurious yet simple to make.

Materials

Fabric for frill
Fabric for edging (or bias binding)
Fabric for cushion cover
Toning or contrasting thread if required
Cushion pad
Zip

Measuring up

For the cushion cover, *see page 53*. For frills, measure round the cushion and double the figure to get the total length required. Cut three strips cut across width of fabric, each about 4cm (1½in) wide for Bound-edge frill and about 11cm (4¼in) wide for Double frill. For a Single frill strips should be about 5cm (2in) wide. For deeper frills simply add the extra depth to the above measurements, remembering that these include seam allowances.

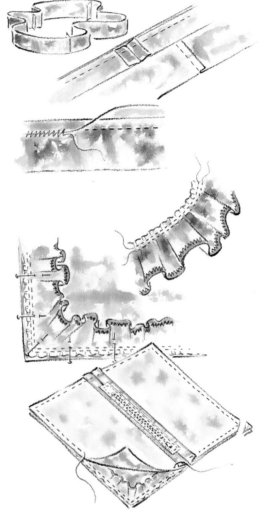

Making up

Bound-edge frill

1 Join ends of strip in French seams *(see page 118)* to form a circle.

2 Cut edge strips to same length as frill, each 2cm (¾in) wide. Join ends in plain seams. (If using bias binding add 4cm (1½in) for turnings.)

3 Lay edging along edge of frill, right side of edging to wrong side of frill, and sew 6mm (¼in) seam all round, turning edging in to neaten. Fold edging up over seam allowance to right side of frill and machine satin stitch over raw edge of edging. Run two lines of gathering around the raw edge of frill and gather to fit cushion.

4 Pin gathered edge to edge of front of cushion cover, right sides together *(see page 54, across back, or page 55, zip across back)*, place back over front with zip open and right sides together, and sew 1.5cm (⅝in) seam round. Trim seams, turn right sides out, unpick gathering and press.

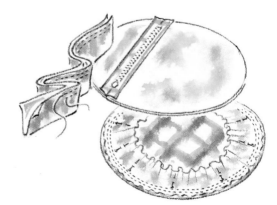

Ready-made Trimmings

Ready-made trimmings

There is a wide variety of ready-made trimmings, ranging from braid and ribbon to decorative cords, fringing and lace. These are generally straightforward to apply.

These types of details often create a period feel and add an extra note of richness to rooms with a traditional flavour.

Decorative cord

Measuring up

Measure all the edges to be decorated with cord and add an extra 5cm (2in) for join.

Materials

Fabric for cushion cover with zip in seam *(see page 54)*
Cord
Zip

Fringed Edges

Fringes usually have some kind of heading, so simply make up a cushion cover with whatever closing you like (see pages 53-55), and carefully hand sew fringing to finished cover along heading. When arranged togther, fringed cushions can create a warm, welcoming feel.

Making up

1 Make cushion cover as zip in seam cover *(see page 54)*, leaving a small gap in a central position on one side of the cover (at bottom if design faces one way or a side other than side with zip).

2 Tuck 2.5cm (1in) of one end of the cord in the gap and hand sew the cord along the seam. Tuck the other end into the same gap, join the cord together where the ends cross with tiny stitches on the outside and stitch the join to the fabric.

Cushions 60

B o l s t e r

The bolster, a traditional supporting cushion, was once a common feature on beds. It is well suited to tailored divan beds or to beds used for seating. Its ends can be flat or gathered. If gathered, the centre can be trimmed with a covered button or tassel; if flat, the separate ends can be piped.

Materials

Main fabric
Bolster pad
Two buttons, for covering, or piping (as desired)
Zip 10cm (4in) shorter than bolster (optional)

Measuring up

For Gathered end bolster, you will need a rectangle of main fabric whose depth measures the required circumference of the bolster, adding 3cm (1¼in) for seams, and whose width measures the required length plus the radius of the end and 1.5cm (¾in) at each end. Add fabric to cover buttons (if required).

For Flat-ended bolster, you will need a rectangle whose depth measures the circumference of the bolster, adding 3cm (1¼in) for seams, and whose width measures the length of the bolster plus 3cm (1¼in) for seams. For ends, you will need two circles whose diameter measures the diameter of the bolster, adding 3cm (1¼in) for seams. For piping, measure all the edges to be piped and add an extra 5cm (2in) for each join.

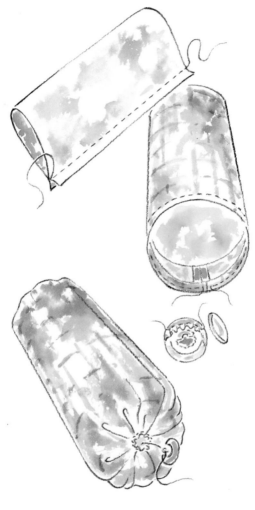

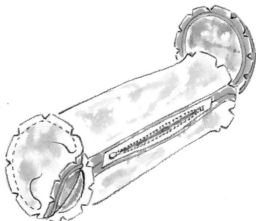

Making up

Gathered-end bolster

1 With long edges together, right sides facing, sew 1.5cm (⅝in) seam. Press open and turn right side out.

2 Turn 1.5cm (⅝in) to wrong side at each end and run a row of gathering stitches along it. Insert the pad – leaving equal fabric at each end – gather ends round bolster and fasten.

3 Cover the two buttons (following manufacturer's instructions) and attach them to centre of each end.

Piped flat-ended bolster

1 Bring long edges of rectangle together, right sides together, and sew 5cm (2in) long 1.5cm (⅝in) seams in from each end. Tack opening along seam line.

2 Press seam open, lay zip wrong side up along tacked part of seam and sew neatly into place. Undo tacking and open zip.

3 See page 121 for piping instructions. Place circle for end at end of main piece of bolster, matching edges, and sew 1.5cm (⅝in) seam all round. Snip notches into seam allowance. Repeat for other end of bolster, then turn right side out and press.

After window treatments, upholstery is probably the next most common application of fabric in the home. Chair and sofa covers, sprung cushions and padded seats can be treated in a variety of ways, some of which are within the scope of the amateur and some of which are not. Tailored upholstery, or 'close covering', especially on large-scale pieces such as sofas and armchairs is a job best left to the professional upholsterer. But there are a variety of other simpler and small-scale treatments which can be carried out by a confident amateur. And, in any case, an awareness of the range of options will enable you to choose upholstery fabric with greater flair and to decide on the style you want.

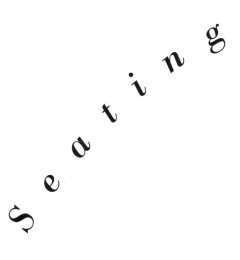

Seating

of the piece giving it an elegant, tailored look. Piped trim will further accentuate form, acting as a frame to a picture and providing a neat and stylish finishing touch.

Pieces which have a simple outline, or those which are upright or square-backed, often look good in loose covers which hang in soft folds or finish in a pleated skirt. Loose covers have the additional advantage of being easy to remove and clean. And they can be changed from season to season, alternating, for example, a rich winter pattern with a plain light summer set of fabric covers.

Choosing fabric

Draping furniture with a length of fabric in an informal way can be a stylish temporary solution when you are considering what sort of permanent effect you would like to achieve. Fine woven blankets, quilts or throws add textural interest and supply extra warmth and comfort. Lengths of plain or dyed cotton sheeting draped or knotted in position will transform a worn sofa or armchair, creating a clean modern look which goes well with bare wooden floors, simple white walls and plenty of bright natural light.

Before committing yourself to an expensive purchase, it is a good idea to try out upholstery fabric by borrowing a sample from your supplier, draping it over the piece of furniture and living with it for a while. This will enable you to assess how the pattern and colour of the fabric work with the other elements in the room and will make sure that you don't make any hasty, potentially costly decisions that you could regret later.

As with curtain fabric there is a wide range of upholstery fabric available, in patterns which range from traditional chintzes and paisleys to fine satins and brocades, geometrics and modern prints. All-purpose upholstery fabrics include stripes, mattress ticking and plain cotton calico, all of which have an innate freshness particularly suited to clean-looking contemporary interiors.

Seat upholstery

Most of the upholstery jobs which can be easily executed at home involve making tailored seat covers and cushions. These can transform old wooden or basket chairs, plain bench seating and the type of furniture which, while it is not a precious antique, still has character.

Whether or not you actually carry out the work yourself, the style of seat upholstery merits careful thought. You should consider not only the type of fabric, colours and patterns, but also the way in which it fits the furniture and how it is trimmed.

A chair or sofa with strong curving lines can benefit from close covering to reveal the shape

Window Seat

left *Window seats can be easily created with a simple box cushion and embellished with a bolster at either end.*

Upholstered Divan

opposite top *A bed upholstered in a rich trellis design is decorated with a collection of cushions and throws, creating an interesting mixture of colour and texture.*

Day Bed

opposite bottom left *Simple checks and plain fabrics in blue blend together on a day bed to provide a contemporary feel.*

Upholstered Ottomans

opposite bottom right *Ottomans are a good way of adding extra seating to a room without taking up too much floor space. They can be upholstered with material that matches or complements the other fabrics used.*

Simple Seat Cushion

Wicker garden furniture, old chairs or sofas and many junk shop buys often need extra padding to make them comfortable. This simple method is ideal for covering a seat cushion, oblong of foam or seat pad. Only one piece of fabric is needed. The opening is slip-stitched, not zipped, but can be unpicked easily for cleaning. For a piped edge, like that shown in the photograph, you will need a separate top and bottom piece, with the piping attached to the top before it is stitched to the bottom *(see pages 56 and 121)*.

Materials

Main fabric
Foam, seat pad or cushion

Measuring up

You will need a long rectangle of fabric whose depth measures the circumference of the foam, adding 3cm (1¼in) for seam allowances, and whose width measures the length of the foam, adding half its depth and 3cm (1¼in) for seam allowances.

Seat cushion with piped edge

To make a seat cushion with a piped edge like the one opposite, cut out two rectangles whose depth measures halfway down one side of foam plus depth of top surface of foam, plus depth of other side of foam, adding 3cm (1¼in) for seam allowances, and whose width measures to these same points on the length of the foam, not forgetting seam allowances. Small tucks are made at the corners of top and bottom pieces to fit neatly over corners of foam, piping is sandwiched between top and bottom pieces, *(see pages 56 and 121)*, seam is sewn all round, leaving gap to insert foam. Cover is turned right side out, foam is inserted and the opening is slip-stitched closed.

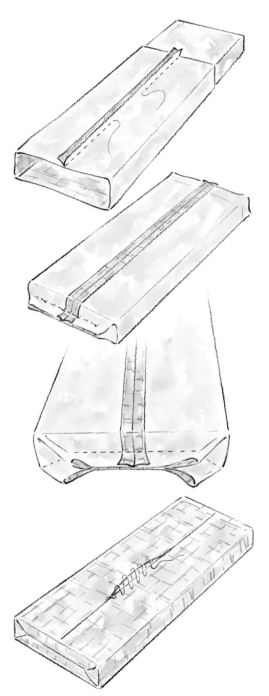

Making up

1 Bring the short edges together, right sides together, and sew 1.5cm (⅝in) seams in from each end, leaving an opening in the centre large enough to slip foam through.

2 Press the seam open and slip the cover over the foam, wrong side out so that the fabric overhangs each end by the same amount. Pin ends together halfway up depth of foam, pinch each corner of cover together to form diagonal lines meeting the horizontal pinning and pin. Repeat for other end.

3 Remove cover from foam. Stitch end seams and short diagonal seams to form mitred corners.

4 Trim seams, clip corners, turn right side out and slip cover over foam. Slip-stitch the opening closed.

Piped Box Cushion

Deep chairs, such as wicker basket chairs, need correspondingly deep cushions to be truly comfortable. This box cushion has a gusset to accommodate its depth neatly. It can be square, round or cut to the exact shape of the seat. Bear in mind that it is easier to insert the cushion if the opening in the cover extends round the back corners a little way.

Materials

Main fabric
Foam or cushion pad
Piping, purchased or made yourself *(see page 121)*
Zip length of side of foam, adding 7.5cm (3in)

Measuring up

You will need two squares, each measuring same as top of foam, adding 1.5cm (⅝in) all round for seam allowances. For the welt, cut out five sections as shown in diagram, extending the back section for 5cm (2in) along the adjoining sides and allowing 1.5cm (⅝in) extra for seam allowance on all edges including the narrow strips at the back.
You will need enough piping to go round top and bottom edges of foam and 5cm (2in) for each join.

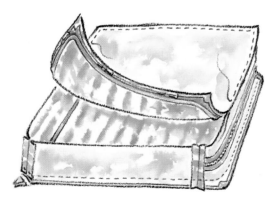

Making up

1 Lay the two pieces of the back strip, right sides together, and sew 2.5cm (1in) long 1.5cm (⅝in) seams in from each end. Tack opening along seam line.

2 Press seam open, lay zip wrong side up along tacked part of seam and sew neatly into place from the right side *(see page 119)*. Undo tacking and open zip.

3 Stitch the ends of the gusset strips together to form a circle, joining the two shorter strips to each end of the fourth strip and the first strip between the two shorter strips. Check that resulting ring fits closely round the foam.

4 Pin piping to top and bottom pieces placing join at back *(see page 56)*.

5 Pin edges of top to edges of gusset, right sides together, and sew 1.5cm (⅝in) seam all round. Repeat for bottom piece.

6 Trim seams, clip corners, turn right side out and press flat.

Simple wooden chairs are unpretentious and appealing, especially around an old, scrubbed table in a country kitchen. Tie-on cushions add a degree of comfort and look cheerful made in fresh checked gingham or a brightly sprigged cotton and piping in a contrasting tone or complementary colour adds a crisp outline.

The covers are cut to the shape of the chair seat and filled with a thin layer of foam. Ties secure the cushion in place. Cushions can also be trimmed with a frill, as long as gaps are left to accommodate the chair uprights.

Materials

Main fabric
Foam, 4cm (1½in) thick
Piping, purchased or handmade *(see page 121)*
Tracing paper

Measuring up the Piped Cover

You will need a paper pattern for the seat cushion top and base which is made in the following way. Lay the tracing paper over the chair seat and trace around the edge. Fold the paper in half from side to side to ensure that the pattern is even and cut it out. Place pattern on chair to check fit and mark the position of the outer uprights. Cut out two pieces of fabric using the pattern, adding 1.5cm (⅝in) all round and transferring the positions of the uprights to the fabric in pencil or sewing tailor's tacks.
For the ties you will need two strips of fabric, each measuring 60 x 2cm (24 x ¾in). Alternatively, you can use ready-made ties or ribbons.
For the piping you will need enough to go round the top piece of the cover and an extra 5cm (2in) for the join in the piping.

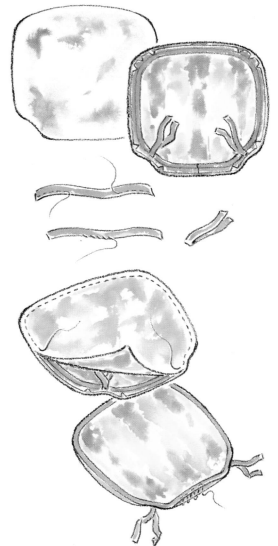

Making up

Piped cover

1 Pin piping to top piece of cover, joining it at the back *(see page 56)*.

2 Fold each strip in half lengthways, right sides together. Stitch across each end and a little over a third down ties' length from each end with 6mm (¼in) seam allowance, leaving an opening. Turn right side out through opening and slip-stitch it closed.

3 Fold each tie in half and stitch them to the seam allowance between the marked positions on the top cover, stitching back and forth several times.

4 Lay bottom piece on top, matching edges, right sides together, and sew 1.5cm (⅝in) seam starting just before one tie and ending just after the second, leaving an opening along back edge.

5 Trim seam and turn right side out through opening. Insert foam and slip-stitch opening closed.

Measuring up the Frilled cover

Follow the instructions for measuring up the Piped tie-on chair cushion (opposite). You will also need fabric for the frills. Cut two strips to the depth of frill you want, adding 4.5cm (1¾in) for seam allowance and hem, making the first strip the length of measurement from outside edge of one outer upright, round front of chair to outside edge of other outer upright plus half again, plus 6cm (2⅜in) for hems, and second strip the same depth as first but length of measurement from inside edge of one outer upright, along back of chair to inside edge of other outer upright plus half again, plus same amount as first for hems.

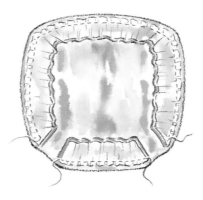

Making up

Frilled cover

1 Turn under 1.5cm (⅝in) along long edges of strips, turn under again, stitch and hem ends of strips in same way.

2 Run a row of gathering stitches along long raw edges and gather first strip to fit first measurement round chair and second strip to fit second measurement. Pin and tack together edge to the top of the cushion cover, with right sides together.

3 Make up the frilled cover in the same way as for Piped cover, beginning at stage 2 and ending at stage 5.

Covering a table with a piece of fabric is the simplest of all soft-furnishing ideas. At the same time it can be extremely effective. Practically speaking, table-cloths are designed to protect fine finishes – or conceal poor ones; aesthetically, they can coordinate or contrast with the decorative scheme, introduce new colour or texture, or emphasize a particular period or mood. Table-cloths are also a good way of trying out different fabric ideas without committing oneself to the relative permanence of made-up curtains or upholstery.

Traditionally, the dining table is most likely to be covered with a cloth. However, side tables, dressing tables and even coffee tables can all be dressed up with fabric. Mats, napkins and table runners offer yet more opportunity for colour coordination or pattern contrast.

Tables

Table-cloths are one area of soft furnishing where you can afford to experiment and try out new ideas. Conventionally, table linen is always tastefully subdued, dressing tables are flounced and frilled, occasional tables have long full-skirted cloths and matching or coordinated overcloths. All of these looks are perfectly acceptable but they are also safe and expected. You don't have to search too hard to find other options which are more exciting and imaginative and also easy to achieve.

One way of updating the skirted cloth and overcloth look for occasional tables is to use a heavier fabric, such as a tapestry or damask. Allow the fabric to drape in rich folds onto the floor. Alternatively, stop the cloth at a three-quarter length if the table legs are worth displaying to full advantage.

On a rectangular table, a narrow runner across the centre would look fresher than an overcloth, providing a hint of Arts and Crafts style. A damask cloth with a runner on top would also be a good tailored solution for a dressing table, especially when combined with a mahogany framed mirror.

Low tables, such as coffee tables, can also be covered with heavy fabrics or even old quilts and kelims. This can be a good way of introducing pattern and texture in a contemporary room; equally, 'table carpets' were a feature of the earliest interiors and can work well in period rooms. Practically, this is also a stylish way of disguising a cut-down junk-shop table.

Dining tables offer even more creative scope. Here it is a good idea to respond to different times of day and different seasons. Clean, clear colours suit summer lunches; warm, rich shades look good by candlelight on autumn or winter evenings.

Dressing a table adds to the festive spirit of any occasion, so set the mood by using colour and pattern. Think in terms of the entire composition, from napkins and place-mats to crockery, the food you will be serving and the flowers decorating the table. As you gain confidence, you can mix patterns and styles. Flowered mats would work well with a black and white checked cloth. Alternatively, every place mat could be in a different floral print, or you could set the table with odd napkins, all with the same edging. This type of simple variation sets an informal tone which is very welcoming and hospitable. For more formal occasions, simple drawn-thread cloths or old damask are more original than lace and are extremely effective.

Table Settings

Creating table-cloths, napkins and place-mats from fabrics that reflect your tableware could not be easier. Experiment with colour, pattern and choice of fabric, and vary your table linen according to the season and the time of day.

left An ornate, floral plate is echoed in the fabric of the table-mat.

opposite Checks are used here as the main theme for an inviting table setting.

Simple Table Linen

Table linen which is intended for everyday use should be made out of washable fabrics. These can include linen, furnishing cotton, gingham, dress fabric and the better synthetic blends such as polyester and cotton mixtures. Ideally, choose a fabric which is wide enough to avoid the need for a join across the table.

Table-mats and napkins can be made out of the same fabric as the table-cloth or from a contrasting or coordinating pattern or colour. All can be edged and trimmed in the same fashion, either by simple fringing, which involves no sewing, or edge-bound or hemmed and satin stitched.

Measure up by following the instructions below, and choose an edging from those described on this page and on page 78.

Measuring up

For the table-cloth you will need to measure the table-top and then decide how far the cloth should hang down (normal depth would be to just above the seat of the dining chair).

Napkins, which are usually square, can be any size you like, from 30cm (12in) to 60cm (24in), so decide which size you want. Plan for the most efficient use of fabric, working out how many napkins can be cut from a width. A good average size is 40cm (16in), adding 1.2cm (½in) hem all round, which is convenient for cutting from 90cm (36in) wide fabric. For the table-mats, decide the size and shape you want – square, rectangular, round, oval – by experimenting with paper templates. Lay a standard place setting, measure the space it occupies and cut out sheets of paper to this size. Average sizes are 30 to 40cm (12 to 16in) for rectangular mats and 25cm (10in) for round, but if the fabric is patterned with a large motif, you may want to adjust sizes to include a complete pattern – as with napkins, though, it is a good idea to choose a size that will divide evenly across the width of the fabric. Add to this enough for hems or borders if required.

Fringed table linen

1 Using an even-weave fabric, cut the table-cloth, napkins and mats to the required size, keeping in line with the pattern.

2 Pull out side threads with the aid of a pin until a fringe of the required depth has been created.

Simple table linen – table-cloths, napkins and mats – can be easily and effectively transformed when bound-edged, finished with an embroidered strip or fringed *(see page 77)*. This creates added interest and provides decorative detailing.

Embroidered borders of a single colour provide simple decoration on a collection of table linen that is made with fabrics of different colours and patterns. Applying embroidered borders to a series of individual napkins and table-mats provides an individual touch and a unifying element.

Alternatively, bound edges and standard hems can be used. Making a set of heat-resistant mats for your table is also a good idea if you are making a complete set of table linen. Since ordinary cloth table-mats are not heatproof, you can easily make your own heat-resistant ones by sandwiching heat-resistant material between two layers of fabric and enclosing the raw edges with bias binding *(see page 120)*. Top stitch through all the layers to finish.

Materials

Main fabric
Contrasting or coordinating fabric for bound edges if required
Embroidery thread for edging if required
Heat resistant interlining for mats if required
Bias binding if required

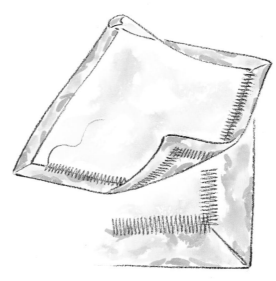

Embroidered Edge Napkins

above *These decorated napkins provide a neat alternative to the fringed table-linen illustrated on page 77.*
opposite *Here white embroidered edges on black checks and black embroidered edges on white backgrounds both unify and emphasize these striking floral fabrics.*

Making up

Embroidered edge napkins

1 Cut out your napkin shape, adding a 1.2cm (½in) seam allowance all round.

2 Fold in edges and machine satin stitch in place to form a decorative border.

Table linen with standard hem

1 For table-cloths, add 2cm (¾in) all round when cutting out. Turn under 1cm (⅜in) along each edge and press. Turn under same again and machine stitch or hand hem into place. Alternatively turn under 2cm (¾in), press and machine satin stitch, enclosing raw edge.

2 For napkins and placemats, add 1.2cm (½in) for hems. Turn under hem allowance to wrong side, press and fold diagonally at the corners. Machine satin stitch enclosing raw edge. Alternatively, turn under 6mm (¼in) to wrong side, turn under same again and machine stitch.

Table linen with bound edges

1 Buy enough binding or make your own *(see page 120)* to go round all four edges, adding 2.5cm (1in) for overlap to length of each strip.

2 Lay binding on table-cloth napkin or mat, right sides together and sew along crease. Bring it up over seam allowance to wrong side and slip-stitch into place, covering machine stitching and folding overlaps round corners to wrong side to neaten.

Formal Table-cloths

Formal or dress table-cloths can be made from fabric which is more luxurious, such as damask – anything, in fact, which will help to create a sense of occasion. Lined cloths also have a certain quality. If contrasting fabrics of the same weight and content are chosen, the cloth will be reversible.

For table-cloths which have a purely decorative use, such as cloths used to cover occasional or coffee tables, you can choose heavy fabric which will hang in quite deep folds. Decorate the edges with a ribbon border.

Materials

Lined table-cloth with bound edges

Main fabric
Contrasting or coordinating fabric for lining
Purchased bias binding approximately 6cm (2⅜in)
  wide or sufficient coordinating or contrasting
  fabric to make your own *(see page 120).*

Decorative Cloth

Main fabric
Contrasting or coordinating fabric for lining
Ribbon or braid

Measuring up

See page 77 and cut main fabric and lining to the same finished size, allowing for 1.5cm (⅝in) seam allowances all round for the decorative cloth.
For bias binding, cut four lengths to match sides of cloth, adding 2.5cm (1in) for overlap to each length.
For ribbon or braid, cut a single piece the total length of the sides of cloth, adding a little extra for ease and neatening ends.

Making up

1 Lay main fabric on lining, wrong sides together; tack all round. If cloth is large, lock pieces together *(see page 117).*

2 If making binding, turn under 1.5cm (⅝in) to wrong side along each edge and press. Bring folded edges of purchased or own binding together and press again.

3 Using 'open' method *(see page 120)*, bind sides of the cloth (shorter sides first), leaving 1cm (⅜in) at each end of long seams unsewn. Use tiny stitches for a reversible cloth. Turn overlaps to lining side and slip-stitch them closed.

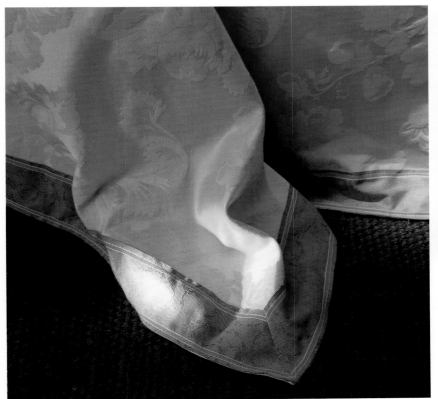

Formal Flair

opposite *A lined table-cloth with bound edges gives a sophisticated table setting.*

left and above *This decorative cloth made from rich Golden Damask fabric provides a luxurious backdrop for a display of objects.*

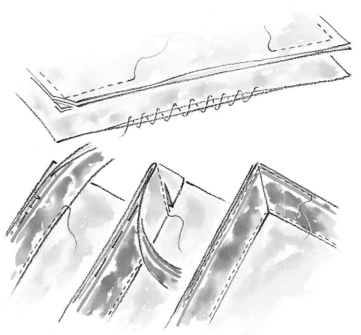

Making up

1 Lay the main fabric on the lining, right sides together, then pin and tack edges. Sew 1.5cm (⅝in) seam all round, leaving an opening to turn cloth to right side. Trim seams, clip corners and turn cloth to right side. Press and slip-stitch closed.

2 Starting in one corner, tack edge of ribbon or braid to edge of cloth on main fabric side down one edge. Top stitch inside edge of ribbon to cloth, stopping short of corner by width of ribbon.

3 Fold ribbon back on itself and sew a 45° seam from inner edge of ribbon, where you stopped top stitching, into point of corner at outer edge, sewing through all thicknesses. Trim folded part of ribbon to 6mm (¼in).

4 Open ribbon and the corner is now mitred. Repeat for remaining sides but for fourth corner, simply cut ribbon on diagonal into corner with 6mm (¼in) allowance, turn under and slip-stitch.

5 Machine top stitch outer edge of ribbon all round, undo tacking and press.

The bed has always been a place to display fine fabric. In the past an elaborately dressed and decorated bed was the ultimate status symbol and upholsterers went to great lengths to design canopies and drapery for their wealthy clients. State bedrooms and the bedrooms of the rich were public places; today, however, the bedroom is a private retreat. But it remains a place where fabric can convey a sense of comfort, warmth and intimacy.

Bedrooms have also traditionally been viewed as 'feminine' places and decorated accordingly, with frills, bows, cascades of lace and pretty floral patterns. Many people still find this type of look attractive but without careful handling it can be a little claustrophobic. It is equally effective to use fabric in a more tailored way. One particular advantage of this approach is that it enables the bedroom to be used for reading, letter writing and sewing, easing the pressure on space.

The bed is the natural focal point of the bedroom, but one which can be overly dominant without clever use of soft furnishings. In most bedrooms, the bed occupies a considerable amount of floor area, so it is important to break up the expanse visually, using cushions, throws and blankets.

If you want to make use of the bedroom during the day, opt for a strong, tailored look, dressing the bed so that it looks more like a sofa or daybed. Pile cushions at both ends, keep the cover simple and add woven blankets or throws for textural interest. A plain reversible cover made from two complementary fabrics is better than the heavily quilted traditional spread which can convey too much of a 'bedroom' atmosphere. If you place the bed lengthways against the wall it can be more readily adapted as seating during the day.

Bed curtains were once a practical necessity, providing warmth and privacy, as well as an excuse to display sumptuous fabrics and trimmings. Few people today have either the space or the inclination for grand bed treatments featuring canopies and draw curtains. But a less elaborate look and one which is relatively inexpensive to create can be achieved by making narrow curtains for each corner of the bed which hang from a simple, topless frame and do not draw. These recreate something of the drama of a four-poster without the claustrophobia or bother.

The bedroom is also the place for all kinds of fabric accessories – fabric bags and boxes for storing shoes, hats, laundry, lingerie, scarves and linen. Covering boxes with fabric provides the opportunity for coordinating pattern and colour, supplying additional storage in a very attractive yet practical way.

Bedroom Choices

These three beds all reflect a careful choice of fabric and furnishings to suit the room.
above A Biedermeier bed is decorated with historically accurate bolsters.
right Subtle shades of blue are used on bed linen that blends with floral bed curtains.

Country Style

opposite A delicate country feel has been created by using a clever mix of summer shades – blue, pink and green – on a delightful rustic bed.

Bed   Curtains

Purely decorative, each of these attractively lined, bound-edge curtains measures only one fabric width across and is loosely gathered by hand. There are six curtains in all: one pair for each side of the bed and one pair for the foot, and they are attached with ties.

Materials

Main fabric
Lining fabric
Contrasting fabric for edging
Heavyweight iron-on interfacing
Ribbon or tape, if desired

Measuring up

For the curtains and lining, measure from the fixing point (such as the top of a bar or the bottom of wooden curtain rings) to the floor, adding 7.5cm (3in) for the stand-up heading. If you want the curtains to bunch on the floor a little, add an extra 15cm (6in) to this measurement. Use the full width of the main and lining fabrics. You will need sufficient of both main and lining fabrics to accommodate these dimensions six times. For the edging, you will need four strips of contrasting fabric for each curtain, each measuring 6cm (2¼in) wide, two measuring the length of the curtain and two its width, adding 2cm (¾in) for neatening the ends.

For each curtain you will also need a strip of interfacing measuring the width of the curtain and 10cm (4in) deep. You will need a strip of lining fabric for the heading measuring 12.5cm (5in) deep and the full width of the fabric for each curtain.

You will need fabric (say, the lining fabric) for the ties. Each tie is made from a strip of fabric measuring 6cm (2¼in) wide and 46cm (18in) long. You will need enough of these strips to fix at 7.5cm (3in) intervals along the top of each curtain.

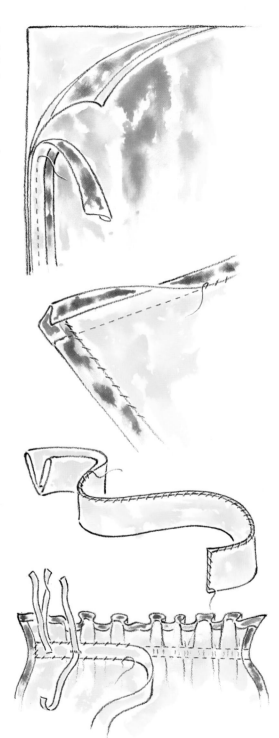

Making up

1 Lay strip of interfacing on wrong side of main fabric 1.5cm (⅝in) down from top edge and iron into place.

2 Lay lining on main fabric, wrong sides together, aligning edges and checking that it is perfectly flat. Pin and tack within seam allowance round all edges.

3 Prepare binding strips *(see page 120)*. Attach binding to long, then short edges of curtain as shown, turning in overlaps on short strips.

4 Run two lines of hand gathering along top of curtain, one 6.5cm (2½in) down from top edge, the other 2cm (¾in) lower. Draw up threads and tie off. Space gathers evenly.

5 Trim heading strip to gathered curtain width. Turn under 1.5cm (⅝in) to wrong side along ends and 3cm (1¼in) along sides, press, bring folded edges together and press again. Sew folded edges together. Pin heading strip to lining side of curtain over gathering stitches. Slip-stitch into place.

6 Make up ties with 1.5cm (⅝in) turnings. Fold each tie in half and sew to heading strip at 7.5cm (3in) intervals.

Reversible Quilt

Quilting is both a decorative and a functional technique, securing layers of fabric and wadding together in a pattern of stitching that traditionally is hand-worked but can easily be machined using a quilting foot.

A quilt provides an extra layer of warmth in the winter over other bedding. Alternatively, for a lightweight summer cover, you can dispense with the wadding and simply quilt the two layers of fabric together.

The pattern of quilting is most effective if it reflects the pattern of the fabric. Wide stripes can be accentuated by quilting lines following the lines of the stripes; bold patterns or motifs can be outlined. For plain fabric or small repeats, a small grid of 15cm (6in) squares is very attractive.

Choose fabrics that come in wide widths to avoid having to make joins. If joins prove to be necessary, place one width of fabric down the centre, joining pieces at either side.

Materials

Main fabric
Contrasting fabric
Wadding, if required
Quilting foot

Measuring up

Decide how far down you want the quilt to hang each side of the bed – to the floor or to just below the mattress if you want a valance to show. Taking your measurements over a made-up bed, measure the length, including the pillows and allowing enough to tuck in at the top, and the width, including the desired overhang each side. If you need to join widths, add 1.5cm (⅝in) for seam allowances. You will need enough main fabric to accommodate a rectangle of these dimensions and an equal amount of the contrasting fabric and wadding.

You will also need enough of the contrasting fabric (or main fabric if desired) to accommodate four strips each 6cm (2¼in) wide, two the length of the quilt and two the width of the quilt, adding 2cm (¾in) to these last two strips for turning under.

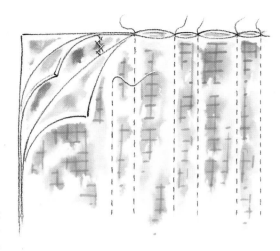

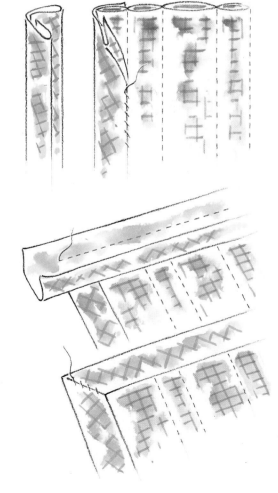

Making up

1 Join widths of fabric if necessary in flat seams, making joins at the same points in back piece.

2 Join widths of wadding by pulling one edge slightly over the other and join with loose herringbone stitch *(see page 116)* over the join.

3 Lay back wrong side up on a flat surface, lay wadding on top, aligning edges, and lay front right side up on top, again aligning edges. Starting at centre, pin and then tack all three layers together across width of quilt at 10cm (4in) intervals, working long running stitches. Finally, tack all round edge within seam allowance.

4 Quilt your chosen pattern, sewing each line in opposite direction to the one before it to prevent fabric slipping and puckering, using quilting foot.

5 Prepare the binding strips *(see page 120)*. Trim edges of quilt even if necessary, open out the long strips and apply by the second method shown on page 120.

6 Attach the two shorter strips to each end of quilt in the same way, but leave 1cm (⅜in) overhanging each end and turn this round bound edge to back of quilt before slip-stitching into place on back. For a really professional finish, stop sewing binding seam where it meets other binding seam and then tuck end of binding under diagonally from seam to outside corner before taking it over to the back and carefully slip-stitch the fold into place to give a mitred effect.

Pillowcases

As with cushions, pillowcases offer an excellent opportunity to add interest and detail with different types of trimming. Choose fabrics that complement or contrast with the main pattern of the duvet cover or coverlet, or pick out a single shade to give some visual relief in a coordinated scheme.

The style of trimming should accord with the overall design of the room: lace edging for a frilly look, bound edges or flat borders for a modern, clean-lined effect, ribbon or tie closures for a pretty, old-fashioned scheme.

Plain pillowcase

Materials

Wide sheeting fabric

Measuring up

Measure the length of the pillow and double it, adding 21cm (8½in) for the flap and hem allowance, then the width, adding 3cm (1¼in) for seam allowances. You will need enough fabric to accommodate this long rectangle across its width.

Pillow Edgings

Lace edging in heavy cotton or broderie Anglaise *can be used to trim pillowcases, adding a particularly luxurious and fresh look.*

To display an intricate lace design, apply the lace without gathering it, but just adding a little extra fabric to pleat it around the corners.

For a gathered frill, allow for fabric to be twice the perimeter of the pillowcase.

Pillow Borders

*A flat border on a pillowcase
complements a highly patterned
fabric with its simplicity,
although it can be embellished
with lines of decorative
machine stitching if desired.*

*A bound-edge pillowcase
looks especially attractive if the
binding strips are cut from a
coordinating fabric, either
plain or patterned. The strips
are cut on the straight grain of
the fabric.*

Making up

1 Make a double 6mm
(¼in) hem along one of
the short sides.

2 Turn under 5cm (2in) to
wrong side along other
short side, press, tuck under a
1cm (⅜in) hem along raw edge
and sew into place.

3 Lay pillowcase out flat,
wrong side up, and fold
over the narrow-hemmed side
to make a 15cm (6in) deep
flap. Press and pin edges
together carefully.

4 Fold pillowcase in half,
wrong sides together,
aligning edges. Pin, tack and
sew long side edges in 6mm
(¼in) seams.

5 Turn pillowcase out so
right sides are together
and sew a second seam down
each side 1cm (⅜in) in from
first. Turn right side out.

Duvet Cover

A duvet cover is one sewing project that everyone can make, whatever level of sewing skill you possess. The fabric should obviously be machine-washable; polyester/cotton or all-cotton sheeting is very practical and comes in generous widths which means you can avoid having to make joins. You can choose two different colours or patterns for the top and bottom to make a reversible cover or trim the edge with a frill or lace border *(see page 121)* for extra interest. There are a variety of options for fastening. These instructions are for press fastener tape; alternatively you could use Velcro, individual press fasteners, a zip *(see page 101)* or ties.

Materials

Main fabric
Second fabric, if desired
Press fastener tape

Measuring up

Duvets generally come in one of several standard sizes: single, 140 x 200cm (54 x 78in), double, 200 x 200cm (78 x 78in), and king size, 220 x 230cm (86 x 90in). You will need enough material for double the measurements of your duvet, adding 1.5cm (⅝in) on the sides and top for seam allowances and 8cm (3¼in) at the bottom for closing.
You will also need a length of press fastener tape measuring the length of the bottom edge of your duvet. Make sure that the tape is 3cm (1¼in) longer than the opening.

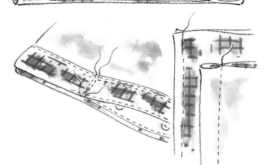

Making up

1 Cut out two rectangles to required measurements. Sew a double 2.5cm (1in) hem at each bottom edge.

2 Lay front on back, right sides together. Make short seams at bottom edge as shown – 30cm (12in) long for a double duvet, 15cm (6in) for a single stitch fastener tape to opening edge.

3 Bring hems together and, on wrong side, sew two vertical seams to enclose raw edges of fastener tape. Sew the seam again for strength.

4 Turn cover so wrong sides are together, aligning sides and corners and work French seams *(see page 118)* down each side. Work French seam along top edge in same way and press.

Valance

A valance is a gathered skirt that is sewn onto a flat piece of fabric which covers the bed base under the mattress. Normally coordinated with the duvet cover or coverlet, its purpose is to hide the base of the bed from view and give the bed a finished appearance. If the flat section of the valance will not show, cheap lining fabric or calico can be used, especially if the skirt fabric is expensive. Alternatively, cotton sheeting is a good choice for the whole valance.

Materials

Main fabric
Lining or calico for flat section, if required
Plate (as template for curved corners)
Pencil

Measuring up

You will need a rectangle of the main fabric, lining or calico whose sides measure the length and width of the bed base, adding 3cm (1¼in) to the width for seam allowances and 3.5cm (1⅜in) to the length for seam allowance and hem.

For the skirt you will need a strip of the main fabric whose width measures the depth from the top edge of the bed base to the floor, adding 6.5cm (2⅝in) for seam allowance and hem, and whose length measures twice the total measurement for the two sides and the end of the bed base, adding 1.5cm (⅝in) for seam allowances every time you need to join fabric to make a strip this long.

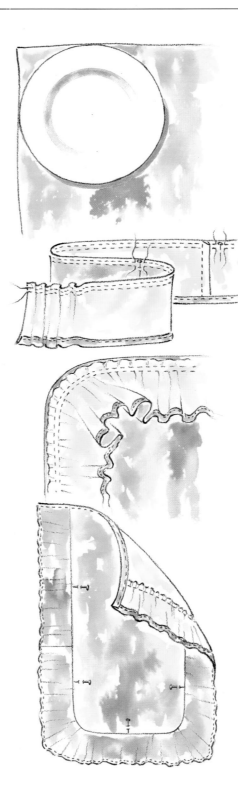

Making up

1 Cut out the rectangle, rounding off the two corners that will sit at the end of the bed by drawing around the plate and trimming off the corners.

2 Join the skirt strips using French seams (see page 118).

3 Turn 2.5cm (1in) up to wrong side along bottom edge of skirt, press, turn up same again, press and machine hem.

4 Fold the skirt into six equal sections, marking each fold with a pin at the top edge.

5 Run two rows of gathering between the pins in each section within the seam allowance and then gather up.

6 Divide the measurement for the total of the two sides and the end of the bed base by six and mark this measurement with a pin round edges of fabric rectangle.

7 Lay skirt on rectangle, right sides together, aligning raw edges and pin on both skirt and rectangle. Adjust gathering so each section fits exactly, then tack.

8 Sew 1.5cm (⅝in) seam and sew again within seam allowance slightly away from first line of stitching. Trim seam and machine zigzag along edge to neaten. Press seam in towards rectangle.

9 Turn 1cm (⅜in) in to wrong side along side edges of skirt and remaining raw edge of rectangle, press, turn under same again, press and machine hem.

The Moses basket is a nursery classic and makes an excellent and portable bed for very young babies, up to three or four months old.

Cotton is the best fabric for the liner, or any of the better, washable cotton blends. If the fabric is patterned, the outer lining should be cut lengthways from the material to avoid joins, with only the inner piece cut from the fabric. If there is no pattern, both pieces of fabric can be cut lengthways.

To fit out the basket, buy a closely fitting safety mattress to lay over the base made of combustion – modified foam conforming to safety regulations.

Materials

Main fabric
Contrasting fabric for top trimming
Mediumweight wadding
Paper and pencil

Measuring up

To work out how much fabric you will need, collect the following measurements for the basket:
Circumference of top edge and depth of basket at deepest point, adding 3cm (1¼in) for seam allowances and at any joins.
Two ovals for the base, adding 1.5cm (⅝in) all round for seam allowance.
For top trimming, four strips 16.5cm (6½in) wide and length from handle to handle at both ends, and between handles each side, adding 76cm (30in) to each for ties. To neaten liner edge at handle joins, measure length of join, adding 2cm (¾in) for turning in and allow for four strips 5cm (2in) wide.
Allow for binding strip 4cm (1½in) wide and length of circumference of base plus 2cm (¾in) overlap (*see page 120*). You will need enough wadding to match the dimensions of liner.

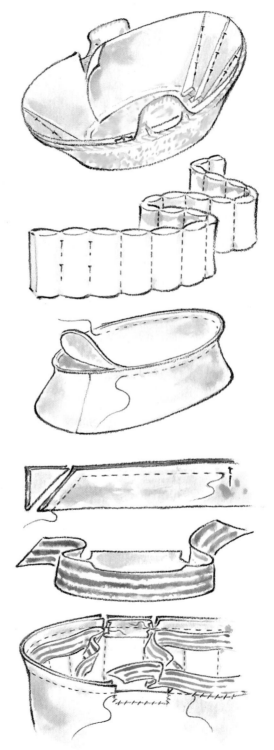

Making up

1 Cut two strips from the main fabric to the first measurements left. Join strips as necessary with 1.5cm (⅝in) seams, leaving final seam unsewn for the moment. Cut a strip from the wadding to same measurements. Cut two ovals from main fabric for the base. Cut out top trimming strips from contrast fabric and four small strips and the binding from main fabric.

2 Lay one of the side strips inside basket, right side facing basket, seam allowance of lower edge turned onto base, ends overlapped. Trim any excess from sides following shape and cutting 1.5cm (⅝in) above edge. Trim second strip and wadding to shape.

3 Pin darts in fabric to take up excess fullness. Tack darts, machine and press.

4 Machine stitch down dart seams on fabric side, then work machine quilting at 10cm/4in intervals along rest of strip (*see page 117*). Checking fit again, stitch final seam of liner. Trim wadding close to stitching.

5 Pin and tack other strip round quilted ring, matching top edge and taking in little tucks as necessary to fit at bottom edge. Turn in overlapping end along seam allowance, slip-stitch closed.

6 To make base, machine the fabric ovals together, wrong sides facing. Stitch base to ring as shown, with 1.5cm (⅝in) seam. Trim seam to 1cm (⅜in).

7 Fold 1cm (⅜in) in to wrong side down each edge of binding strip and press. Bring folded edges together and press again. Bind seam to neaten.

8 For top trimming, press 1cm (⅜in) to wrong side along long edges of strips. Fold and pin each strip in half lengthways, right sides together, cutting ends

to a point as shown. Pin edges together. Measure 38cm (15in) in from each end of each strip, mark with a pin. Sew 1cm (⅜in) seams out from pins to ends and down diagonals to points.

9 Snip into seam allowance at pin positions through only one of layers. Turn strips right sides out. Press with clipped

layer folded out and unclipped layer folded to inside. Slip liner into basket. Pin trimming strips around inside of liner, right sides together, aligning snipped ends of seam allowances with edges of handles. Remove and tack. Snip into seam allowance of liner to correspond to snipped edges of trimming strips. Sew 1.5cm (⅝in)

seams through all thicknesses.

10 Press 1.5cm (⅝in) to wrong side down long sides of four finishing strips. Neaten seam allowance at handle joins with strips as shown, turning in ends and slip-stitching to outside of liner. Bring folded edges of trim strips to outside of liner and slip-stitch. Slip liner into basket, turn over contrast trim and tie.

C h a n g i n g   M a t

Eminently practical, an essential baby accessory when you are on the move, this travelling changing mat incorporates a fold-up towelling surface for changing a baby's nappy on, together with a compartmentalized pocket for keeping cotton wool, spare nappies, cream and clothes. The towelling is backed with fabric and ties up neatly with fabric ties. To make your mat truly practical, choose a backing fabric that is washable.

Materials

Towelling
Main fabric
Lining fabric
Contrasting fabric for ties, if desired
Paper and pencil
Saucer (for use as a template)

Measuring up

You will need enough towelling to accommodate one of the pattern pieces above.

You will need enough of the main fabric for one of the pattern pieces and 20cm (8in) of the bottom of the pattern again for the pocket, plus enough to make 6cm (2¼in) wide binding (see page 120) to go round the edges of the mat, adding 2cm (¾in) for neatening ends, and along the top edge of the pocket (you could bind the edges with the contrasting fabric if you prefer.

You will need the same amount of lining as you did of the main fabric for the pocket.

Of the contrasting fabric, you will need enough for four strips, each 6cm (2¼in) wide and 35cm (14in) long. (If you are using the main fabric for the ties as well, simply add this amount to your calculations for the amount of main fabric you will need to buy.)

Making up

1 Make your paper pattern as in the diagram left, using the saucer to round off the corners.

2 Cut out one piece from the towelling and one from the main fabric. For pocket, pin the bottom edge of the pattern to the main fabric and cut along bottom and 20cm (8in) up each side, cutting final side of fabric horizontally. Cut one piece from lining fabric. Cut out and make up bias edging strips from main or contrasting fabric (see page 120) as desired and cut out strips for ties from main or contrasting fabric.

3 Lay the main fabric piece right side down, lay the towelling piece over it, aligning edges and curves, and tack loosely within seam allowance all round edge. Lay the pocket piece and its lining wrong sides together and tack.

4 Prepare binding (see page 120) and cut a length to fit the top edge of the pocket. Attach as shown on the left.

5 Lay pocket main-fabric-side up on towelling side of mat, aligning raw edges, and tack round sides and bottom. Tack a vertical line 10cm (4in) in from each side and machine stitch along tacking through all thicknesses, stopping at binding and sewing back and forth at end a few times for strength. These form the separate sections of pocket.

6 Turn mat over and pin binding all round edges, right sides together, aligning raw edges, stretching it slightly to fit round the curved corners. Turn overlapping end under

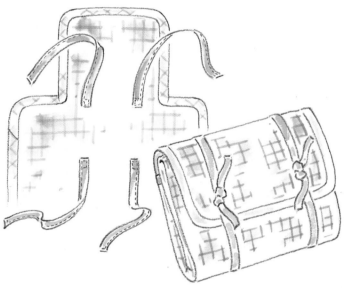

neatly and machine stitch 1.5cm (⅝in) seam all round, through all thicknesses. Bring binding up over seam allowance to towelling side and slip-stitch to towelling very neatly, covering line of machine stitching and enclosing all raw edges. You will need to make small tucks in binding at inside curve of each corner and gently stretch and ease binding over curved seam allowance for a neat fit.

7 To make the ties, fold 1.5cm (⅝in) to wrong side down each side of each strip, press, bring folded edges together and press again. Fold

in ends, then machine stitch across ends and down length of each strip.

8 Lay the mat fabric-side up on a flat surface and measure 6cm (2¼in) in from each inset corner, along foldline for flap. Pin a tie at each of these points with free ends lying on flap. Then measure 13cm (5in) down from these points and pin the other two ties in place.

9 Machine-sew ties in place at all the pinned positions, sewing a small square shape through all thicknesses several times. This provides added strength.

Quick Change

This highly practical portable changing mat is very easy to make and incorporates useful pockets for accessories such as cream, cotton wool and spare nappies. When not in use it folds away neatly and is secured with integral fabric ties. Use stripes or checks that complement the fabric used on the Moses basket.

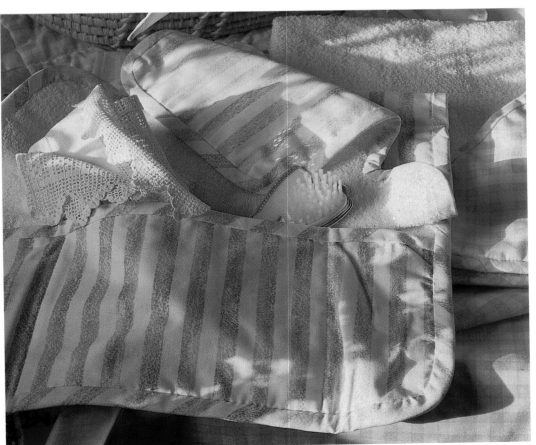

Nappy or Towel Holder

This hanging fabric bag is for storing nappies or towels. It is suspended from ties fashioned into a bow. The base of the bag is stiffened with a piece of thick card, and a short wooden lath in the casing at the top keeps the holder in shape. The sides of both the base and top casing are just slip-stitched closed so that the card and lath can easily be removed when you want to wash the holder.

Materials

Main fabric
Contrasting fabric for casing
Thick card
Wooden lath

Measuring up

Cut a rectangle from the card 19 x 30cm (7½ x 12in). You will need enough of the main fabric to accommodate two rectangles this size, adding 3cm (1¼in) to their length and width for seam allowances. Then measure round the edges of the card rectangle and subtract 4cm (1½in) as you will need a rectangle of main fabric whose width measures this amount and whose length measures 60cm (24in) or longer if desired. You will also need enough contrasting fabric to make binding strips for the shorter sides of this large rectangle, each 6cm (2¼in) wide.
You will also need enough of the contrasting fabric to cut out a piece measuring 10 x 33cm (4 x 13in) and two pieces each measuring 3 x 25cm (1¼ x 10in) for the ties.
You will also need a lath 2.5cm (1in) wide and 30cm (12in) long.

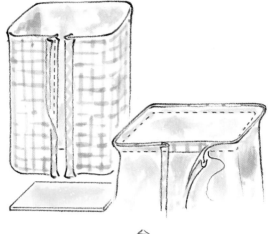

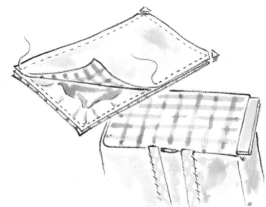

Making up

1 Bind short sides of large rectangle of fabric (*see page 120*).

2 Pin bottom edge of large rectangle to one of the smaller rectangles, right sides together, leaving a 4cm (1½in) gap between the bound edges at the middle of one of the longer sides. Sew 1.5cm (⅝in) seam from bound edge to bound edge.

3 Fold the large rectangle down as small as possible so it sits within the edges of the base. Lay second small rectangle over folded fabric, right side down, aligning edges and corners, pin and sew 1.5cm (⅝in) seam along long sides and one shorter side, leaving fourth side open. Clip corners and trim seams. Turn right out, slip card rectangle through open seam and neatly slip-stitch closed.

4 With holder sitting on stiffened base, hold top so bound edges meet and lie on the centre of back. Flatten so fold each side aligns with midpoint of each short side of base, then pleat as shown until top edge overlaps wooden lath by 6mm (¼in) at each end. Pin and tack within seam allowance; press pleats and folds as far down as you can.

5 Make ties with 6mm (¼in) turnings. Pin in place each side of top edge of holder.

6 Prepare casing strip with 1.5cm (⅝in) turning. Stitch to top edge of holder as shown, turning in overlaps.

7 Insert wooden lath and then neatly slip-stitch ends together until closed.

Hanger and Dust Cover

Display tiny clothes to full advantage by hanging them on padded hangers that are protected by matching fabric covers.

Materials

Main fabric
Contrasting fabric for binding dust cover
Mediumweight wadding
Strong adhesive
Child-size hangers

Measuring up

For padded hanger, you will need a long strip of fabric 1.2cm (½in) wide to cover hook, and enough wadding to wind around hanger. You will also need a rectangle of fabric the length of padded hanger and wide enough to wrap around it, adding 2cm (¾in) for seam allowances.

For dust cover, measure two pieces of main fabric the length of padded hanger, plus 13cm (5in), by 20cm (8in). You will also need contrasting fabric for binding strip 6cm (2¼in) wide and long enough to bind edges of cover.

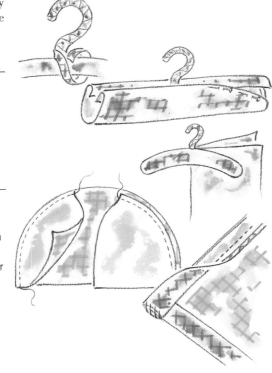

Making up hanger

1 Apply adhesive to hook. Fold strip in half lengthways and wind around hook, securing ends. Wind wadding round hanger and secure.

2 Fold rectangle of fabric in half lengthways, wrong sides together, turning 1cm (⅜in) seam allowances in along top edges. Pin one side round hanger, trimming to follow shape exactly.

3 Pull other side up to overlap first edge. Trim and tuck under. Slip-stitch seam neatly.

Making up dust cover

1 Make pattern for back and fronts to measurements above, to suit hanger shape. Cut out fabric.

2 Stitch fronts to back with 1.5cm (⅝in) seams. Bind bottom, then front edges.

Baby Towel

The hooded baby towel is made from a square of towelling with a corner pocket of fabric lined with towelling to form the hood. Other plain towels and flannels can be made to match by cutting them to the required size, binding the edges and attaching loops to hang them up.

Materials

Towelling
Fabric for hood and binding
Small plate

Measuring up

You will need enough towelling to accommodate a 90cm (36in) square and a triangle with two 23cm (9in) sides and a 32cm (12½in) hypotenuse.
You will need a triangle of fabric same size as triangle above for hood.
You will also need enough fabric to make bias binding *(see page 120)* 6cm (2¼in) wide to bind all four edges of towel, adding 2cm (¾in) for neatening ends, edge of hood and 10cm (4in) to make loop.

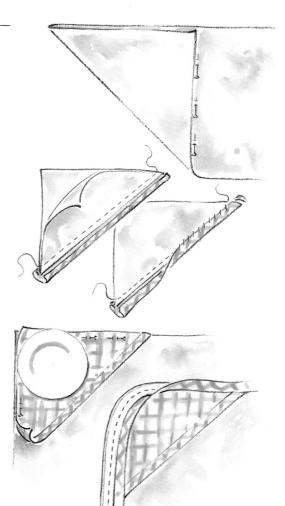

Making up

1 Cut a square from the towelling as shown, and cut triangles from the towelling and fabric. Round off the square corners by trimming round the plate.

2 Lay two triangles together, wrong sides facing, matching edges and tack within seam allowance.

3 Prepare the binding *(see page 120)*, then cut a length measuring same as longest edge of triangle. Bind the long triangle edge as shown.

4 Lay triangle in one corner of square of towelling, fabric-side up, aligning raw edges of triangle and square and tack together within seam allowance.

5 Cut length of binding sufficient to bind edges of towelling square and, with hood uppermost, lay it along edges, right side of binding down, stretching it slightly to ease round corners, turn under overlapping end and sew 1.5cm (⅝in) seam all round.

6 Bring binding up over seam allowance to other side and slip-stitch to towelling, covering line of machine stitching. Ease binding round curves to fit if necessary.

7 To make loop, machine stitch along folded edges of remaining binding, fold the strip in half and stitch the ends, folded under, to the edge of the back of the towel halfway down one side.

Cot Duvet Cover

This cot duvet cover is made using two contrasting fabrics and is fastened with fabric ties. The top has an inner flap like a pillowcase to tuck the duvet into and make a neater tied edge.

The duvet and its cover would make a lovely first birthday present as it is not advisable for a baby to sleep under a duvet until he or she is 12 months old; a very young baby could easily suffocate if placed under a duvet.

Materials

Main fabric for top
Contrasting fabric for base and for ties

Measuring up

Measure your duvet. The standard size is 100 x 120cm (39 x 47in). You will need enough main fabric to accommodate these dimensions, adding 23cm (9in) to the length and 3cm (1¼in) to the width. You will need enough contrasting fabric to the same basic size adding 4cm (1⅜in) to the length and 3cm (1¼in) to the width.
You will also need enough of the contrasting fabric to accommodate four strips, each 6cm (2¼in) wide and 18cm (7in). long.

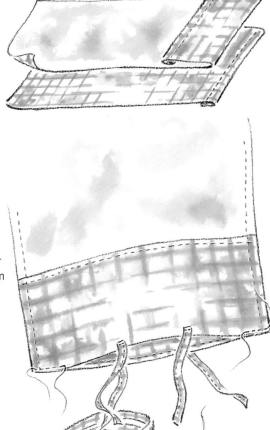

Making up

1 Turn 1.2cm (½in) to wrong side along one of shorter sides of the base piece, press, turn under same again, press and machine stitch into place.

2 Neaten same edge of top rectangle as above, then lay it wrong-side up on top of the other rectangle, aligning sides and raw end, and fold up neatened end so fold aligns with other neatened edge and press.

3 Turn this rectangle so wrong sides are together, raw edges and folded and hemmed edges aligning and sew French seams down each side (see page 118). Repeat for top edge.

4 With right sides together, sew 10cm-(4in-) long seams in from each end of flap end close to edge, leaving a central opening.

5 To make the ties, fold 1.5cm (⅝in) in to wrong side down each side of strips, press, bring folded edges together and press again. Open out ends of each strip, fold in 1.5cm (⅝in), close and press. Machine stitch across ends and down side of each strip.

6 Pin two of the ties to inside edge of opening of cover, spacing them equally, and machine stitch several times for strength. Attach the other two ties in the same way to the same points on the other edge.

Cot Quilt

Patchwork makes a cheerful addition to any bedroom, but its bright geometric patterning is particularly sympathetic in a nursery. True patchwork, hand sewn from scraps of many different materials, is an heirloom, but a very effective alternative can be made quickly and easily using a sewing machine.

Choose about three or four fabrics which work well together. They should also be the same weight and type and washable. Use graph paper and coloured pencils or crayons to devise a simple pattern from the squares.

The size of the finished quilt is dependent on the size and number of patches. This one is based on 10cm (4in) finished squares. For a standard cot, seven patches wide by nine down is about right.

Materials

Three or four fabrics for patches
Lining fabric
Fabric for binding edges
Mediumweight wadding

Measuring up

You will need enough of each fabric to cut out the required number of patches of that fabric to make up the pattern you want, each patch measuring 12cm (4¾in) square.

You will also need a rectangle of the lining fabric measuring the desired finished size of the quilt.

Of the fabric for binding the edges of the quilt, you will need sufficient to accommodate four strips each 6cm (2¼in) wide, two measuring the length of the quilt and two the width, adding 3cm (1¼in) to the two shorter ones for neatening the ends.

You will need to use the same amount of wadding as lining fabric.

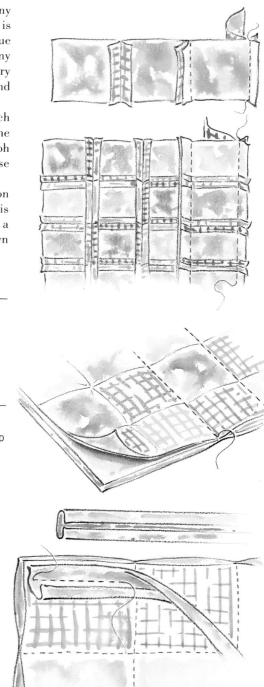

Making up

1 Lay patches on flat surface as you want finished quilt to be. Pick up the top-left-hand patch and the patch directly beneath it, lay right sides together and sew 1cm (⅜in) seam. Press seam open. Continue in this fashion until all patches for left-hand edge have been joined together to form a long strip. Take care to keep seam allowances exact.

2 Continue across 'quilt' in same way until you have sewn all the patches together in long strips.

3 Pick up first and second strips and lay right sides together, aligning right-hand edge of first strip with left-hand edge of second strip and horizontal seams, and sew 1cm (⅜in) seam. Press seam open.

4 Continue across 'quilt' in same way until all strips have been joined together in correct order.

5 Lay lining right-side down on flat surface, lay wadding on top, aligning edges and corners, and lay patchwork right-side up on top, aligning edges and corners, and tack all round edge within seam allowance. Then tack along seam lines of patchwork, from the centre out.

6 Machine-sew along seam lines of patchwork using a quilting foot if available *(see page 117)*, sewing along length of quilt first, starting with the middle seam, then either side of that and so on, then across width, starting with the middle seam and working out from the centre as for stage 5.

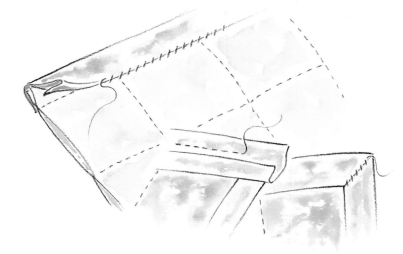

7 Fold 1.5cm (⅝in) to wrong side down each side of binding strip, press, bring folded edges together and press again. Cut two lengths to fit length of quilt and two to fit width, adding 1.5cm (⅝in) overlap at each end.

8 Lay the longer strips along each side of quilt on patchwork side, right sides together, aligning edges, and sew 1.5cm (⅝in) seam through all thicknesses. Bring binding up over seam allowance to lining side and slip-stitch.

9 Sew the two shorter strips to top and bottom edges in the same way, but leave equal overlaps at each end and, at each corner, stop seam at edge of binding for sides and turn under overlap diagonally front and back and slip-stitch closed to form neat mitred corners.

Fabric accessories are the ultimate in room coordination. As you apply the fabric in a natural way, the result will never be fussy or twee. Simple drawstring bags – for lavender, laundry or shoes – are a good way of practising sewing skills.

Fabric can also make a feature out of ordinary storage boxes. A stack of fabric-covered hat boxes or show boxes adds a fresh touch to a bedroom while banishing clutter. Basket liners and padded hangers pursue the upholstered look.

In the living room, fabric details can contribute to a period atmosphere. Fabric bows suspending pictures or miniatures have an eighteenth-century appeal while fabric-covered screens supply a sense of drama.

Accessories

One simple idea which can be very effective is to cover storage boxes with fabric that complements the rest of the room's furnishings. Hat boxes, which look attractive stacked in different sizes, are much the best way of storing hats. Shoe boxes can also be fabric-covered and used to keep a whole range of bedroom clutter from view. Choose fabrics which are sympathetic to the rest of the decoration, but avoid slavish coordination which can look overpowering.

The fabrics are simply stuck in place with fabric glue. Roller blind stiffener can be applied to the edges before gluing the fabric pieces to the box. This stops the material fraying and eliminates the need to turn the edge under, avoiding a bulky edge.

Hat Box

Materials

Main fabric
Hat box
Fabric glue
Roller blind stiffener, if required
Tape
Cord, if required

Measuring up

You will need a rectangle of fabric to go round the sides of the box whose length is circumference of box, and whose width is height of box, adding 5cm (2in) for finishing bottom edge.
To cover lid, place lid on fabric, draw round it and cut out fabric, to lie just short of the lid's edge.

Shoe Box

Materials

Main fabric
Shoe box
Fabric glue
Roller blind stiffener, if required

Measuring up

You will need two squares of fabric whose sides measure same as ends of box, adding 5cm (2in) to the width and 7.5cm (3in) to the depth. For the sides you will need two rectangles of fabric whose length is just short of each end of the box (if not using fabric stiffener, add 2.5cm/1in) and whose depth is depth of box, adding 7.5cm (3in). For the lid you will need a rectangle of fabric whose sides measure the same as the top of the lid, adding double the depth of the sides of the lid to each side.

H a t   B o x   a n d   S h o e   B o x

Hat Box

Making up

1 If using stiffener, apply it to edges of fabric that is going to show on finished box and let it dry.

2 Stick long rectangle of fabric around box, aligning one edge with top edge of box, and overlap ends.

3 Snip into excess fabric along bottom edge at regular intervals, spread glue to depth of overlap on base of box and fold snipped edge onto glue, square by square. Seal edges with tape once glue is dry.

4 Take lid, stick the strip onto the edge, letting same depth of fabric overhang to line inside edge and the rest to overhang other side to fold onto top.

5 Snip into both overhanging edges at regular intervals. Spread glue on inside edge and fold snipped edge onto glue, square by square. Repeat for lid top.

6 Stick the circle of fabric for top of lid to lid, covering snipped edges. Let glue dry, then stick to lid top.

7 If you want, you can add a cord handle. To do this, punch holes in each side of box and thread through a contrasting cord, knotting the ends on the inside.

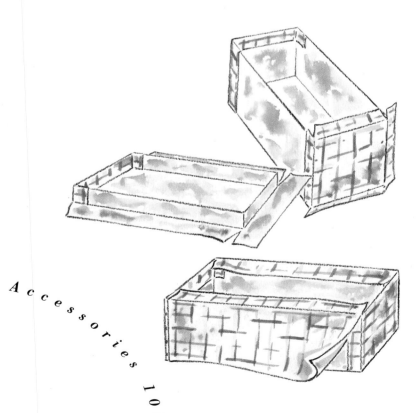

Shoe Box

Making up

1 Stick the ends onto the box first, checking that they are on centrally with equal overlaps at top, bottom and sides. Make vertical cuts into overlap at corners on top and bottom edges. Spread glue along inside top edge, outer sides and along bottom edge of box to depth of overlap, standing box on its end. Press side edges in place first, press top edge to inside of box and bottom edge to underside.

2 Stick sides to sides of box, checking that tiny gaps at each end and overlaps at top and bottom are equal. Spread glue along inside top edge of box to depth of overlap, turn-in fabric and press down along both top edges. Stick overlaps along bottom edges in the same way.

3 Lay the fabric for the lid right-side down on a flat surface, spread glue on top of lid and place it on fabric with equal overlap all round. Snip into overlap of side edges to corners.

4 Spread glue along sides and inside sides of box lid, bring up overlaps at end, fold over edge and press inside, overlapping around the sides, trimming to neaten where necessary.

5 Bring overlaps up sides of lid, fold over edge and press inside.

P i c t u r e   H a n g e r

In the eighteenth century, silk bows and ribbons often hid the cords and hooks which suspended pictures from picture rails. This charming decorative flourish, which works especially well in traditional rooms, can add emphasis to a fine mirror or painting or help to unify a series of miniatures or small pictures hung vertically.

The fabric itself is not used to hang the picture, but simply disguises the means of suspension. You can fix the picture directly back to the wall and hang the false hanger from the top, or run the fabric along in front of the real cords and tie it in a bow to cover the hook. Rosettes are also a common embellishment for this type of decorative detail.

Crimson silk or ruby velvet were fabrics seen in the original authentic treatments, but any rich furnishing fabric will create a similar effect. The fabric needs to be lined.

Materials

Main fabric
Lining of contrasting or coordinating fabric

Measuring up

Measure the length required and decide what width best suits the position. You will need a strip of main fabric cut to these measurements, adding 1cm (⅜in) all round for seam allowances.

For lining you will need a strip cut to the same measurements, but 2cm (¾in) wider (the picture hanger illustrated is made of an 11cm/4¼in wide strip of main fabric attached to a 13cm/5in wide strip of lining fabric).

Making up

1 To achieve desired length of strip, you are likely to need to make one or more joins. Join with French seams *(see page 118)* across the straight grain of the fabric.

2 Place the main fabric and lining strips right sides together, matching raw edges, pin and stitch 1cm (⅜in) seams along both sides.

3 Turn out to right side and, with main fabric uppermost, adjust to see 5mm (¼in) of lining along each side and press.

4 Cut a V-shape and slip-stitch closed so lining border matches sides or finish as desired.

5 Pass finished strip through a loop on the frame, tie and fasten to the wall as illustrated.

Envelope Bags

This basic and easy-to-sew bag is made from one piece of fabric, folded over itself and fixed with ties. It can be made in any size for any number of purposes – to store lingerie, toiletries, scarves and the like. The exact proportions of the rectangle can also be varied, from a long, slim oblong to a more squared-off shape, to suit whatever you intend to keep in it. Whatever size you make the bag, the point of the V-shaped flap should come about halfway down the front.

Materials

Main fabric
Contrasting fabric for binding *(see page 120)*
Paper
Ruler
Pencil

Measuring up

You will need a piece of fabric that measures two and a half times the depth of the desired size of the finished bag by the desired width of the bag.
You will also need a strip of binding 6cm (2⅜in) wide and long enough to bind top inside edge and from bottom edge of bag to tip of V of flap both sides, adding 2cm (¾in) for overlaps, and enough to make two ties that you can fasten in a bow, adding 1cm (⅜in) at each end for finishing (about 15cm/6in long).

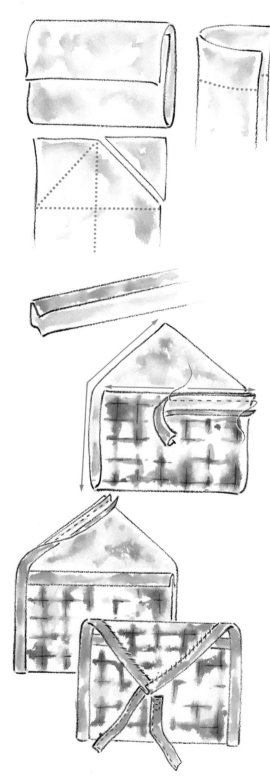

1 Make a paper pattern. Draw the shape of bag you want on the paper. Measure the depth of your shape, halve this measurement and draw a horizontal line this distance above the top edge of your shape. Then draw a horizontal line below bottom edge of your shape, the same distance as depth of your original shape, and extend lines for sides to join up with it. Fold the paper along your two original top and bottom lines. This is how the finished bag folds too.

2 Open out and fold in half lengthways, matching up side lines, to find the centre point.

3 Open out and draw diagonal lines to join the marked folds for the V-shape. Cut all round and you will have two boxes and a V-shaped top.

4 Pin pattern to fabric and cut out. Fold to form bag and press.

5 Make up binding *(see page 120)*. Cut three lengths of binding: one same length as inside top edge and two others, each measuring from folded bottom edge of bag to point of V, adding 2cm (¾in) for overlaps.

6 Open out the first short strip of binding and pin it to top inside edge of bag, right sides together, aligning raw edges. Sew 1.5cm (⅝in) seam. Turn binding to wrong side, turn under edge and carefully slip-stitch into place.

7 Fold fabric to form a bag and tack sides into place within seam allowance.

8 Open out one of the long lengths of binding and pin to front of bag from folded bottom edge to point on V, right sides together, aligning raw edges and leaving 1cm (⅜in) overlap at bottom fold. Trim flush with fabric at V-shaped end. Sew seam through all thicknesses. Slip-stitch to other side as before, turning in overlap at bottom fold.

9 Repeat for the other side, leaving 1cm (⅜in) overlap at V as well, stitching across the other binding at the V, and turning the end in neatly as at bottom folded edge.

10 To make the two ties, cut remaining binding in half, turn in the ends, bring the long folded edges together and machine stitch close to edge and across ends. Stitch one tie securely to the underside of the V. Fold down the flap and stitch the other to the corresponding position on the front of the pocket with several rows of stitching. Tie in a bow to finish.

D r a w - s t r i n g   B a g s

Fabric bags with draw-string closures are very versatile. They can be made in any size to suit a variety of purposes – small bags for lavender or pot pourri, medium sizes for shoes or gym kit, large sizes for laundry.

These bags make attractive presents. They can be trimmed by piping, either purchased or made yourself (*see page 121*), or fringing and a lining can be added if desired.

Basic draw-string bag

Materials

Main fabric
Cord for drawstring
Paper
Pencil and ruler

Measuring up

A small bag might measure 12.5 x 18cm (5 x 7in), a medium one 28 x 40.5cm (11 x 16in), a large one 46 x 66cm (18 x 26in).

Make a paper pattern to the required size, allowing 10cm (4in) at the top for the heading on the small bag, 15cm (6in) for the heading on the larger ones and seam allowances of 1.5cm (⅝in) around the other three sides. You will need two pieces of fabric cut to this size.

For the draw-string you will need two lengths of cord, each measuring twice the width of the bag plus about 15 to 20cm (6 to 8in), choosing cord the thickness of which is in proportion to the size of bag you are making, but no thicker than 1cm (⅜in).

Making up

1 Make a 1.5cm (⅝in) long cut on each side of the fabric pieces to mark allowance for heading (i.e., 10 to 15cm/4 to 6in) down from the top edge).

2 Turn under 1cm (⅜in) to wrong side at top edge of both pieces and press. Turn in 1.5cm (⅝in) on both sides above the cuts and press.

3 Turn down top edge again so that folded top edge meets cuts. Stitch along this line close to edge and again 2cm (¾in) up from this line to form a casing for the cord. Repeat for the other piece.

4 Lay the two together, right sides together, aligning edges and corners, and sew a 1.5cm (⅝in) seam, beginning at one cut, sewing down to corner, along bottom and up other side, ending at other cut. Turn right side out.

5 Thread first cord through front casing from right to left and then through back casing from left to right and knot ends. Pass second cord through casing the opposite way and knot ends so you have a knot each side of bag.

Fringed bag

1 Follow steps 1, 2 and 3 of Basic draw-string bag then pin fringing to bag piece.

2 Ensure centre of depth of finished top edge of fringe lies along seam line and that fringe strands are kept away from seam line. Curve fringing at bottom corners.

3 Continue and finish as steps 3-4 above.

The following pages, which comprise a stitch directory, fabric glossary and list of suppliers, provide all the information you need to turn the ideas presented in the book into reality. The stitch directory covers all the basic sewing techniques, from hemming to inserting a zip, which arise during the course of the projects. The fabric glossary is an introduction to common terms used in the world of soft furnishings. Finally, a list of suppliers of Designers Guild fabrics makes a useful shopping reference to help you locate the fabric you want easily. A comprehensive list of fabrics that appear in the book is also included.

Techniques

Stitches

Backstitch

A firm stitch which is the hand-sewing equivalent of machine stitching.

Bring the needle and thread to the upper side of the fabric. Insert the needle 3mm (¼in) behind this point along seam line, then bring the needle forward and back up to the upper side of the fabric; this should be the same distance forward of the original point through seam line.

Repeat, inserting the needle at the end of the previous stitch each time.

You will know you are working this stitch correctly when the stitches on the underside are twice as long as those on the upper.

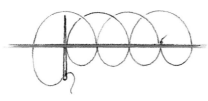

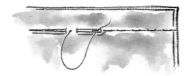

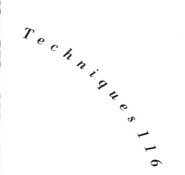

Hemming

For hand sewing a hem.

Work on the wrong side of the fabric. Hold the needle diagonally and pick up a couple of threads from the main fabric close to the folded edge. Then without pulling it through, pass it through the folded edge and then pull through gently to form stitch.

These two parts of the stitch should be worked in one continuous movement. The result will be small, slanted stitches.

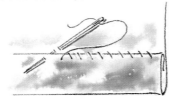

Herringbone stitch

This is a firm hemming stitch suitable for bulky fabrics or for joining wadding.

Work on the wrong side, from left to right (or vice-versa if left-handed), covering the raw edges. Bring the needle up through the hem and take it diagonally across to make a backwards stitch in the fabric just above the hem edge.

Bring the needle diagonally back to the hem again and make a backwards stitch in the hem. Keep the thread fairly loose throughout the procedure.

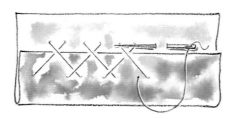

Ladder stitch

A tacking stitch, ladder stitch is very useful when matching two pieces of patterned fabric, as the right sides can be seen together at all times.

Press under the seam allowance on one edge and place this folded edge along the seam line of the other piece so that the pattern matches exactly. Pin into place.

Fasten the thread to the fabric beneath the folded edge and insert the needle into the seam line of the unfolded piece, bringing it back up through the fabric 2cm (¾in) down the seam and pulling the thread through.

Insert the needle into the folded edge at this same point and make a stitch between the two layers of the folded fabric the same length as before, bringing the needle out through the fold.

Insert the needle into the unfolded piece at this same point and continue in this fashion for the length of the seam.

The fabric can then be folded right sides together ready for the seam to be sewn.

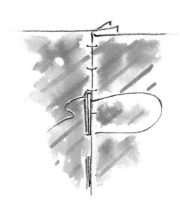

Locking stitch

A loose stitch used to hold lining and interlining to curtain fabric to stop the lining sagging.

Lay the interlining and lining on the wrong side of the curtain so that all the layers are perfectly flat, then pin them together in lines down the length of the curtain equidistant from each other – about 60cm (24in) apart is about right.

Fold the lining back along the first line of pins and, using thread that matches the curtain fabric, work a horizontal stitch in the lining fabric and another at the same point in the curtain fabric, picking up only a couple of threads.

Bring the thread down the fold and make a stitch 5cm (2in) down from the first, laying the thread under the needle before you pull it through, but keep the long thread loose between stitches.

Machine Quilting

Decide on the design you want to quilt marking the shapes in pencil if necessary. Join all the layers with tacking stitches to keep them secure while you are stitching. The lines of tacking should run at right angles to the lines of machine sewing.

Machine sew alternate quilting lines in opposite directions. Using a quilting guide or gauge helps make regularly spaced lines and reduces the need to mark out. Providing the first line of the design is marked and the following lines run parallel to it, you can stitch from the first line without any subsequent guideline.

For padded quilting, you will need to use a quilting foot.

Running stitch

Use this stitch for hand gathering.

Secure the thread with a little back stitch and work small, evenly spaced stitches, simply bringing the needle up through the fabric and back down again. For gathering, work two rows a short distance apart either side of the seam line, leaving threads loose at one end. Slide the fabric along the threads, spacing the gathers evenly, and fasten off the loose ends, if necessary, by winding them round a pin inserted at the end of the gathering.

Slip stitch

This stitch is useful for holding hems in place nearly invisibly on both sides and can be used to stitch down any other folded edge.

Make a tiny stitch in the main fabric, picking up one or two threads, close to the folded edge and, without pulling the thread through, slip the needle into the folded edge opposite the first stitch, bringing it out 6mm (¼in) to the left and pull through. Make the stitches in one continuous movement, keeping the stitches small and neat.

Tacking

These are temporary stitches used to hold fabric in position.

Make a knot in the end of the thread and, working from the right to left, make long running stitches. To remove the stitches when the permanent stitching has been completed, simply cut off the knot and pull the thread. Remember to use fine thread and needle for delicate fabrics.

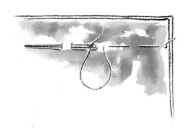

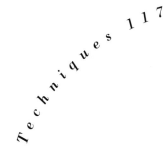

Seams

Basic flat seam

This simple seam is used for joining widths of fabric and in making up most of the projects in this book.

Place the two pieces of fabric to be joined right sides together, unless otherwise instructed, aligning raw edges. Pin and tack just inside seam line. Sew 1.5cm (⅝in) in from raw edges, working a few stitches in reverse at each end to secure threads. Remove tacking and press.

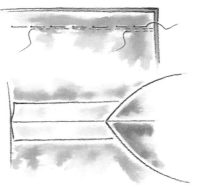

Curved seams

After sewing a curved seam, snip into the seam allowance on outward-facing curves and snip notches into the seam allowance on inward-facing curves. Doing this enables the seam allowance to lie flat when the seam is pressed open.

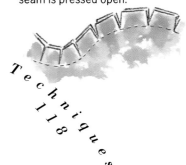

T e c h n i q u e s
1 1 8

French seam

This is a self-neatening seam, but it is only suitable for light fabrics and for joining straight edges. It is a very hard-wearing seam and is often used for duvet covers, pillowcases, laundry bags and the like.

With wrong sides together and edges aligned, sew a seam 6mm (¼in) in from the edge. Press the seam open and trim. Fold the fabric along the seam, right sides together, and sew a second seam 1cm (⅜in) in from the edge, which is the first seam, and the raw edges will be enclosed. Press and turn the fabric to the right side.

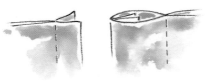

Neatening raw edges

There are several ways of doing this. You can work machine zigzag stitch over the raw edges or, if working by hand, oversew edges so that small diagonal stitches lie over the edge, stopping it fraying.

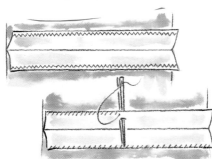

If the fabric is not prone to fraying easily, you can run a line of machine stitching about 1cm (⅜in) in from the edge and then trim the edge with pinking shears.

Sewing corners

To sew a perfect right-angled corner seam, sew up to the corner, stopping with the needle in the fabric 1.5cm (⅝in) short of the edge, lift the presser foot and turn the fabric through 90°, lower the foot so it sits parallel to the raw edge and continue sewing. Finish by snipping across the corner seam allowance.

On sharper corners, sew one or two stitches across the corner – more for bulkier fabrics – and trim the seam allowance by snipping the corner off as before, but trim a little more off each side of the point as well.

When you are joining a strip of binding or piping to a corner, pin and tack it into place up to the corner. Snip into the seam allowance of the binding or piping from the corner so that the snip matches the point of the corner exactly, bend the strip round the corner, pin, tack, then sew the seam as for right-angled corners above.

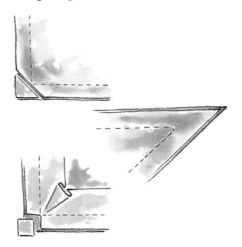

F a s t e n i n g s

Buttons

The following method results in a very professional finish. Fasten the thread to the right side of the fabric where the button is to go. Slip the button onto the needle and place a matchstick on the button and work stitches over it. Remove the matchstick, pull up the button and wind the thread around the slack to form a shank, then fasten the thread off. When the button has its own shank, secure the thread and make about 12 stitches through the shank into the fabric.

Press studs

Sew the ball half to the overlapping fabric and the socket half beneath it onto the other piece of fabric. Make sure that the ball half is positioned at least 6mm (¼in) in from the edge. Work five or six stitches through each hole and sew the socket half down in the same way.

Press stud tape

This is a length of tape with press studs fixed to it at regular intervals and you are most likely to have seen it used to fasten the opening in a duvet cover. It is available in different widths.

Sew the ball half to the top layer and the socket half to the underneath, checking first that both halves match exactly. Pin the tape in place and sew using a zipper foot.

Velcro

This consists of two types of material – one with loops, one with hooks – which cling to each other when they are pressed together. It is available in different widths, weights and colours and in strips of small spots.

Simply hand or machine sew into place.

Zips

Zips are useful fasteners for cushions, chair covers and the like, and are available in either nylon or metal and in a range of weights, lengths and colours.

Centred

Sew a flat seam, leaving a gap for the zip. Press the seam open. Tack along the seam line. Lay the zip wrong side up along the tacked part of the seam on the wrong side of the fabric. Tack then sew it into place from the right side using a zipper foot. Stitch across the ends of the zip too.

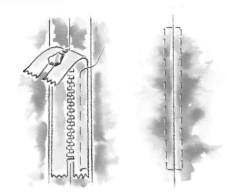

Invisibly inserted in a piped seam

Open zip and lay it face down on right side of the piped seam, with teeth of right half aligning with piping stitching. Tack zip into place then sew along it 3mm (⅛in) from teeth using zipper foot.

Close zip, fold seam allowance back on itself so you see right side of zip, press under seam allowance along other edge and then bring folded edge over zip to meet piping. Tack edge into place and sew 6mm (¼in) from folded edge and across bottom end of zip, stopping at the piping.

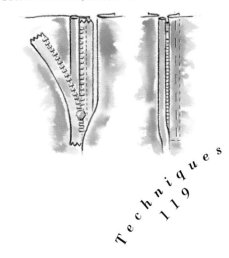

Trimmings

Binding edges

To bind straight edges, use ribbon or strips of fabric cut on the straight grain. On curves, use bias binding, either ready-made or made yourself from fabric.

The width of each strip should measure four times the desired finished width of the bound edge. Fold 1.5cm (⅝in) to inside along each edge, press, bring the folded edges together and press again.

There are two methods of attaching the binding. The first is to place the binding over the raw edge of the fabric so that the centre fold rests on the edge of the fabric, then pin and topstitch through all layers.

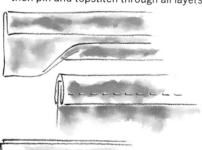

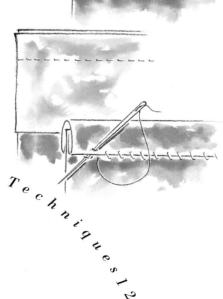

Alternatively, you can apply the binding by opening it out, laying it wrong side up along the edge to be bound, aligning the raw edges and sewing a 1.5cm (⅝in) seam. Then bring the binding up over the seam allowance to the wrong side of the fabric and slip-stitch the folded edge in place, covering the line of machine sewing. This latter method is the one used most often in the making-up instructions in this book.

Making bias binding

Find the bias of the material you are making the binding from by folding the raw edge – cut straight across the grain from selvedge to selvedge – fold down so it lies parallel to one of the selvedges, forming a right-angled triangle. The fold lies along the bias. Draw lines in pencil parallel to the fold the required width of the binding apart. For the projects in this book you will need strips 6cm (2¼in) wide, giving a finished width of 1.5cm (⅝in), but they can be narrower or wider if you wish.

To make binding for covering piping cord, double the seam allowance of 1.5cm (⅝in) and add circumference of cord.

When you need to join strips, work flat seams along the straight grain of the fabric, joining them at right angles, right sides together, then open out the seam, press and trim.

Making a continuous strip of binding

When long lengths of binding are needed, for covering piping for example, strips can be joined before you cut them.

Cut out a rectangle of the binding material that is at least twice as long as it is wide. Find the bias as before but fold the raw edge down to meet the selvedge, cut off this corner and sew it to the bottom edge, right sides together, so that both ends slant the same way. Press open.

Draw the strips in pencil as before but also mark a seam allowance of 6mm (¼in) down each side, that is, along the selvedges. Bring the top-left-hand corner down and round so that the first pencil line in from the edge meets the raw diagonal edge's corner and pin together. Continue down the length of the side, rotating as you go to form a tube with a diagonal seam round it and a strip's width overhanging at each end. The ruled lines must match exactly, so carefully pin and tack right sides together.

Turn to right side to check that lines still meet, then turn back to wrong side and sew a 6mm (¼in) seam. Finally, cut along pencil lines to form one strip.

Piping

Corded piping consists of bias-cut strips of fabric wrapped around special piping cord that is sewn into the seams of soft furnishings.

The larger sizes of piping – ranging from 4 to 6 – are most often used in soft furnishing. Do remember, whatever size you select, to ensure that the cord is preshrunk. Also, when calculating how much you need, measure all areas to be piped and add 5cm (2in) for each join.

To cover the cord, lay it along the centre of wrong side of strip of material, bring raw edges together, aligning them. Pin then stitch close to cord with zipper foot.

Inserting piping

Lay the piping on the right side of one of the pieces to be joined in a seam, with the raw edges aligned and the stitching line along the seam line. Pin it into place, snipping into the seam allowance of the piping at the corners from the corner point.

Sew the piping to the fabric using a zipper foot along the previous line.

Lay the other piece of fabric on top of the piped piece, right sides together, aligning the raw edges, pin and stitch through all layers inside previous row of stitching.

To join corded piping, begin sewing the cord into place 1cm (⅜in) in from the end and stop 5cm (2in) from where you began. Unpick the stitches of the piping binding strip and fold the fabric back. Trim the cord so that the ends abut. Fold the binding fabric back over the cord, fold under the overlapping end and sew into place.

Single frills

Add 1.5cm (⅝in) seam allowance to the desired finished depth and an allowance of 1 to 2cm (⅜ to ¾in) for a double hem. Join strips where necessary with flat seams. Allow 1.2cm (½in) at each end to make a 6mm (¼in) double hem if required.

To finish, turn under the double hem along the bottom edge, and ends. Alternatively bind the edge of the frill *(see page 120).*

Then divide the length into equal sections and run two rows of gathering stitches along the raw edge within these sections. Divide the edge the frill is to be attached to into the same number of sections. Pull the gathering threads up so that the sections of the frill fit the sections of the main fabric. Pin the frill to the main fabric, tack and sew into place.

Double frills

This type of frill gives a fuller look and eliminates the need for a hem.

Cut double the required finished depth of the frill, adding twice the seam allowance. Join lengths where necessary with flat seams. Fold the frill in half along its length, then gather and attach it to the main fabric.

Fabric Glossary

When choosing fabric, check that its weave and weight are suitable for the required use and that it will withstand normal wear and tear. Make a note of its composition, the preferred method of cleaning and its ability to withstand fading or shrinking. Buy enough material to complete the job in question because colours vary from dye lot to dye lot.

Brocade Heavy, traditional fabric with an opulent appearance. Patterned with a raised design, often of stylized flowers, which resembles embroidery. Brocade made of silk was one of the great furnishing fabrics of the past; today, more practically, it is often available in cotton in addition to cotton blends.

Broderie anglaise Dainty cotton fabric with pierced eyelet designs and embroidery, traditionally white. A versatile and fresh-looking edging fabric for bedroom accessories and the nursery.

Calico Firm plain cotton fabric which prints well. Today it is most often used unbleached as upholstery in contemporary rooms.

Chintz Traditional cotton furnishing fabric, originating from India. Typically patterned with bold flowers and birds.

Glazed chintz Is treated with a resin coating to give a dull sheen which repels dust and dirt. The glaze adds extra crispness to the appearance.

Cotton Cotton remains the main soft furnishing fabric, although today it is often blended with artificial fibres such as polyester for extra strength and ease of care. Cotton's ability to take colour well has made it an extremely popular fabric; it is also naturally strong and hard-wearing.

Cretonne Late nineteenth-century furnishing fabric still available today. Made of cotton and similar to unglazed chintz. Cretonne is washable and heardwearing.

Damask Self-patterned fabric with designs woven in. Silk damask has great historical associations and was much used in the Georgian period. Today damask is available in other fibres. White linen damask is popular for table-cloths and napkins. It can be overprinted with a design, supplying an extra textural dimension to prints.

Gingham Fresh, cheerful cotton fabric typically printed with checks in a variety of colours on white. Useful material for creating mixed pattern schemes, since it blends well with many different designs, or can be used on its own in informal settings such as kitchens and nurseries.

Interfacing Iron-on stiffening fabric which gives bulk and rigidity to tie-backs and other fabric accessories.

Interlining Dense soft cotton fabric used to line curtains, thus increasing wearability, deadening noise, blocking light and insulating against heat loss. Interlining is not always attractive: it can create a plump, overstuffed look.

Lace Delicate Filigree openwork fabric, ranging from expensive hand-made work in linen to machine-made designs in modern fibres or cotton. Can be used as a trimming or edging, or hung in flat panels against doors and windows.

Muslin Light gauzy cotton fabric much used in the past for lightweight curtains and window drapery. Economical and effective way of creating special fabric effects.

Sateen Soft blended fabric, often including cotton, with a dull sheen. Typical lining fabric but also used to make curtains.

Satin Fabric with a pronounced sheen on one side. Cotton satin is a practical choice for soft furnishings; bright vivid satins made of silk were popular in Empire and Regency periods.

Ticking Sturdy cotton fabric, very heardwearing, used to cover pillows and mattresses. Increasingly popular as a fresh-looking contemporary upholstery fabric. Woven in narrow black and white stripes.

Wadding Thick cotton or polyester padding available in different weights, used for upholstery and quilting.

Designers Guild Fabrics

The following Designers Guild fabrics appear in this book:

Pages 6 / 7 Top cloth: *Willowherb*, Bottom cloth: *Cavalière*

Page 24 Background and cushion: *Castellane*, Floral chair: *La Verdière*, Cushion: *Montferrat*, Checked fabric: *Castellane*

Pages 28 / 9 Curtains: *Fleurs du Midi*, Seat: *Claviers*, Cushions: *Montferrat*

Page 30 Floral curtain: *Rosebay*, Striped curtain: *Padova*, Chair, left: *Lichen*, Chair, right: *Asiago*

Page 32 Top: *Feuillage*, Curtain, centre: *Rosebay*, Chair: *Manosque*, Bottom, curtains: *Anemone*

Page 33 Curtain, centre: *Provence*, Chair, left: *Castellane*, Chair, right: *Lapalme*, Curtains, bottom: *Spirale*

Page 35 Floral curtain: *Bergamot*, Striped curtain and chair: *Montferrat*

Page 37 Curtains: *Lemon Vine* backed with *Montferrat*, Chair: *Mirepoix*

Page 39 Curtains: *Verona*

Page 40 Top: *Ombrage*, Bottom: *Feuillage*

Page 43 Blinds: *Feuillage*, Chair cushions, centre: *Marguerite*, Wallpaper: *Filigrana*

Page 44 Blind: *Bourbon Rose*, Chair: *Acanthus*

Pages 48 / 9 Main cushion: *Asiago*, Bedcover: *Passariano* backed with *Istrana*

Page 50 Seat and cushion: *Violetta*

Page 51 Chair and cushion: *Damas Fleuri*

Page 52 Cushions, Left: *Montferrat*, Front: *Fleurs du Midi*, Back: *Cavalière*, Right: *Manosque*, Seat Cover: *Claviers*

Page 57 Cushions: *Ornamental Garden Collection*

Page 58 Cushions: *Wild Rose*

Page 59 Main cushion: *Primevère*

Page 60 Yellow cushion: *Damas Fleuri*, Cushion, right: *Mapping*

Page 61 Bolster and bedcover: *Grata*, Sofa: *Rotonda*

Pages 62 / 3 Chair and tie-on cushion: *Tapisserie*, Stool: *Mapping*, Yellow cushion: *Mosaique*

Page 64 Curtain and cushion: *Verona*, Bolster and seat cushion: *Stra*, Chair: *Mantova*

Page 65 Top red curtains: *Brocatelle*, Striped curtains: *Strie*, Bottom right, Ottoman: *Asiago*, Chair: *Passariano*, Bed: *Mosaique*, Wallpaper: *Stucco*

Page 66 Curtains: *Cavalière*, Seat cushion: *Primevère*, Cushions: *Claviers*

Page 69 Blinds and cushion: *Feuillage*, Seat cushion: *Mosaique*

Page 71 Tie-on chair cushion: *Maypole*, Chair: *Strawberry Fair*, Wallpaper: *Field Rose*

Pages 72 / 3 Table-cloth: *Damas Fleuri*

Page 74 Table-cloth: *Verona*

Page 75 Table-mats: *Mirepoix*

Page 76 Table-cloth, bottom: *Manosque*, Napkins: *Mirepoix*, Table-cloth, top: *Claviers*

Page 78 Napkins: *Manosque*, Table-cloth: *Verona* backed with *Mantova*

Page 79 Table-cloth: *Damas Fleuri*, Edging: *Broderie*

Page 81 Napkins, left: *La Verdière*, Napkins, right: *Provence*, Napkins, top: *Primevère*

Pages 82 / 3 Bed curtains and cover: *Rosebay*, Striped cushions: *Passariano*, Checked bed cover: *Istrana*

Page 84 Curtains, above: *Primevère*, Bed cover: *Mandelieu*, Checked cushions: *Cavalière*, Bed curtains, below: *Anemone Stripe*

Page 85 Bed curtains: *Ribbons and Bows*, Bed cover: *Daisy Chain*

Page 87 Curtain: *Primevère*, Bed curtains: *Fleurs du Midi*, Bed cover: *Manosque*

Page 88 Wallpaper: *Balloons*, Curtains: *Wagon Train*, Pillows: *Crosspatch*, Stool, foreground: *Helter Skelter*

Page 91 Large pillow: *Verona*, Curtain: *Castelfranco*, Small pillows: *Stria*

Page 95 Moses basket lining: *Montferrat*,

Page 97 Montferrat

Page 99 Wallpaper: *Balloons*, Frieze: *Hickory Dickory*, Nappy bag, dust covers: *Crosspatch*

Page 103 Curtains: *Dandy Duck*, Cushions, *Crosspatch*

Pages 106 / 7 Hat box, top: *Verona*, Hat box, left: *Monteviale*, Hat box, right: *Bandol*, Shoe box, top: *Mirepoix*, Shoe box, centre: *Manosque*, Shoe box, bottom: *Mapping*, Seat Cover: *Ombrage*

Page 109 Wall fabric: *Claviers*, Picture hanger: *Tamarind*

Page 111 Envelope bags: *Manosque*, Wall fabric: *Streamer*

Pages 114 / 5 Curtains: *Verona* backed with *Mirepoix*

Designers Guild Stockists

Designers Guild fabrics are available from their London showrooms at Designers Guild, 271/277 Kings Road, London SW3 5EN, Telephone: 071 351 5775, and through a comprehensive network of stockists which include those listed below:

A v o n

No. Twelve Queen Street, 12 Queen Street, Bath

NB Interiors, 37 Alma Vale Road, Clifton, Bristol

B e d f o r d s h i r e

Curtain Gallery, 27-31 Greyfriars, Bedford

B e r k s h i r e

Ellis Designs, 12 High Street, Sunninghill

Gallienne Schmidt Interiors and Design, 52 Prospect Street, Caversham

B u c k i n g h a m s h i r e

Clover House at Home of Interiors, 17-19 Frogmoor, High Wycombe

Morgan Gilder, 83 High Street, Stony Stratford, Milton Keynes

Sheridan and York Interiors, 29 Packhorse Road, Gerrards Cross

C a m b r i d g e s h i r e

Design Workshop Watkins & Stafford Ltd, Fitzwilliam Street, Peterborough

C h a n n e l I s l a n d s

Jersey Agencies Ltd, 21 Seale Street, St Helier, Jersey

C h e s h i r e

Designers, 15 London Road, Alderley Edge

Hodges Interiors, West Wing, Chester Station, City Road, Chester

Inspiration 17a Church Street, Frodsham

Jamandic Limited, 22 Bridge Street Row, Chester

C o r n w a l l a n d D e v o n

Casa Fina Interiors, 29 River Street, Truro

The Interior Shop, Castle Lodge, Castle Street, Truro

Ajanta, The Anchor Centre, Kingsbridge

Collingwood Interiors, 17 Wilton Street, Millbridge, Plymouth

Fanfare Interiors, 114 Queen Street, Newton Abbot

G & H Interiors, 1 The Old Pannier Market High Street, Honiton

Harding and Healy, 62 Faraday House Faraday Business Park, Princerock, Plymouth

Hatchetts Interiors Ltd, 3 Cathedral Yard, Exeter

D o r s e t

Dodge & Son, 28 & 33 Cheap Street, Sherborne

Dorchester and West Country Interiors, 2 Nappers Court, Charles Street, Dorchester

House Beautiful, 21 Southbourne Grove, Bournemouth

Individual, 58-60 Poole Road, Westbourne, Bournemouth

Inspiration, 9 Saxon Square, Christchurch

E i r e

Cotton Box Interiors, 21 Middle Street, Galway

E s s e x

Clement Joscelyne Ltd, 9-11 High Street, Brentwood

Epping Interiors, Campion Court, High Street, Epping

G l o u c e s t e r s h i r e

Green Dragon, Sundial House, High Street, Chipping Campden

Maggie Interiors, 6 Montpellier Avenue, The Promenade, Cheltenham

H a m p s h i r e

Norman & Mason's, 16 Osborne Road, Southsea, Portsmouth

The Interior Design Workshop, 39 Jewry Street, Winchester

The Curtain Shop, No 1 Admirals Way, High Street, Hythe

The Drawing Room, 45 High Street, Odiham, Nr Basingstoke

H e r e f o r d s h i r e & W o r c e s t e r s h i r e

John Nash Antiques, 1st Floor, Tudor House, 17c High Street, Ledbury

Allan Vaughan (Interiors) Ltd, 6 Bank Street, Malvern

H e r t f o r d s h i r e

Peter and Susan Brown Furnishings of Distinction, 36 St. Andrew Street, Hertford

Clement Joscelyne Ltd, Market Square, Bishop's Stortford

Champagne (Beautiful Interiors), 117 Crossbrook Street, Cheshunt

Designers Fountain, 20 Heritage Close, High Street, St. Albans

Fishpools Ltd, 115 High Street, Waltham Cross

K e n t

Dineen Designs, 102 Wickham Road, Park Langley, Beckenham

Jenny Dineen Designs, 225-231 High Street, Beckenham

Gordon Larkin, 5/6 St. Margaret's Street, Canterbury

Thorntons Beautiful Interiors, 41-43 Bouverie Road West, Folkestone

L a n c a s h i r e

John Thompson Design Centre, 330-340 Church Street, Blackpool

Home Designs by David Payne Ltd, Andrew House, 1 Lord Street, Wigan Lane, Wigan

Facade Interior Design at the Decoration
Centre Ltd, 52 Woodlands Road, Ansdell,
Lytham St. Annes

Leicestershire

Harlequin Interiors, 11 Loseby Lane,
Leicester

Unique Interiors, 30 High Street, Market
Harborough

Lincolnshire

David Zinnerman, 22 Newland, Lincoln

Pilgrim Decor, 35 Wide Bargate,
Boston

London

Bennett & Cameron, 88 Stoke Newington
Church Street

Chamberlain Furnishings Ltd, 221 Regents
Park Road, London

Harrods, Knightsbridge

Interiors of Chiswick,
454 Chiswick High Road

Liberty Plc, Regent Street

Mr Jones, 175-179 Muswell Hill Broadway

Nova Interiors Ltd, 168 Regents Park
Road, N1

Paine & Co, 49-51 Barnsbury Street, N1

Norfolk and Suffolk

Jeremy & Yvonne Fox (Interiors), The
Studio, Glenone House, School Road,
Frettenham, Norwich

The Granary, 5 Bedford Street, Norwich

Clement Joscelyne Ltd, 16 Langton Place,
Bury St. Edmunds

David Foster Interiors, 67/71 Beech Road,
Rushmere St. Andrew, Ipswich

Edwards of Hadleigh, 53 High Street,
Hadleigh

Nottinghamshire

Nash Interiors Ltd, 17-19 Carlton Street,
Nottingham

Oxfordshire

Pespectives, 3 North Parade, Oxford

Scotland

Decor (Aberdeen) Ltd, 157 Skene Street,
Aberdeen

Designworks, 38 Gibson Street, Glasgow

Grange Interiors, 56 Henderson Street,
Bridge of Allan

Illuminati, 46 Princes Square, on Buchanan
Street, Glasgow

Joni Ancill Interiors, 6 Mains Avenue,
Eastwood Toll, Giffnock, Glasgow

Somerset

Calluna Ltd, Riverside Place, St. James
Street, Taunton

The Curtain Pole, 64 High Street,
Glastonbury

Staffordshire

Archetype, 4 Berkeley Court, Borough
Road, Newcastle Under Lyme

Blythe Interiors, 34a Wolverhampton
Road, Stafford

Surrey

A J Adams Interiors, Baker Street,
Weybridge

Chris Maxted Interiors, 44 Guildford Road,
West End, Nr. Woking

Decorum, 1 Steward House, Sydenham
Road, Guildford

Interior Options, 276 Ewell Road, Surbiton

J Decor Interiors Ltd, 3 South Street,
Epsom

Northover Interiors, 82 High Street,
Reigate

Ideas Unlimited, 10 Russell Hill Parade,
Russell Hill Road, Purley

Sussex

B J Blatcher & Co., 59-63 Broad Street,
Seaford

Geoffrey Furnishings, Swan Corner,
Pulborough

Mister Smith Interiors, 1-3 The Parade,
Croft Road, Crowborough

Pine and Design Interiors, Haywards Heath
Road, Balcombe

Tyne and Wear

Studio Interiors, 4 Old George Yard, Cloth
Market, Newcastle Upon Tyne

Abercrombies, 140-142 Manor House
Road, Jesmond, Newcastle Upon Tyne

Wales

Joni Ancill Interiors, 62 Lake Road East,
Roath Park, Cardiff

Warwickshire

Ladida Interior Design, Union Street,
Stratford Upon Avon

Gramlick Designs, The Coach House,
3a New Street, Shipston-On-Stour

West Midlands

Bennett & Bowman Interiors Ltd, 4 Beeches
Walk, Sutton Coldfield

The Establishment, Enville,
Nr. Stourbridge

Wiltshire

Kembury Interiors Ltd, 71 Manchester
Road, Swindon

Yorkshire

Christopher Pratt & Sons Ltd, 33 North
Parade, Bradford

George Gregg Interiors, Park Road,
Guiseley, Leeds

Martin Stuart, 292-294 Abbeydale Road,
Sheffield

Plaskitt and Plaskitt, 8a Walmgate, York

Sue Rugg Soft Furnishing Design
Specialist, 11 Eastgate, Bramhope,
Leeds

Woods of Harrogate, 65/67 Station Parade,
Harrogate

Australia

Wardlaw Pty Ltd, 230-232 Auburn Road,
Hawthorn, 3122 Melbourne

New Zealand

Mokum Textiles Ltd, 11 Cheshire Street,
Parnell, Auckland 1

Index

Page numbers in *italics*
indicate pages where you will find
photographs or step-by-step
illustrations.

abstract designs, 13, 25
accent, 12, 50
accessories, 12, 33, 84 *see also*
    Baby towel, Bags, Boxes,
    Changing mat, Cushions,
    Hanger, Moses basket, liner
    for, Nappy or towel holder,
    Picture hanger, Pelmets, Tie-
    backs *and under* Covers *and*
    Quilts
Arts and Crafts, 74
Austrian blinds, *see* Festoon
    blinds,
    tracks, 47

baby towel, making, *99*, 100, *100*
back stitch, *see under* Stitches
bags, 84, *see also* Nappy or towel
    holder
    draw-string, making, 112, *112*,
    118
    envelope, making, 110-1, *110-1*
    fringed, 112
bed
    curtains, *see under* Curtains
    linen, *see individual items of
        bed linen*
bedrooms, *20*, 50, 61, *65*, *82-3*,
    84-93, *84*, *85*, *88*, 92, *see
    also* Nursery
bias binding, *see under* Binding
binding, 37, *40*, 41, 44, *44*, *53*,
    59, 77, 78, 80, 81, 86, 89,
    90, *91*, 94, 96, 98, *98*, 99,
    100, 110, *110*, *111*, 118,
    120, *120*
    bias, making, 120-121, *120*
blinds, 19, 29, 31, *32*, *32*, *33*, 38,
    see also Festoon blinds
    Roller blinds, Roman blinds,
    Simple tie blind
blanket, 32, 64, 84
bolsters, *see under* Covers *and*
    Cushions
borders, 50, 58, 90, *91*
    flat double, making, 58, 77, 80,
    58
    embroidered flat, making, 58,
    58, 78
bows, 33, 46, 109
box cushion, *see under* Covers
boxes, 84, *106-7*
    fabric-covered, making, 107-8,
    108
    hat, making, 107-8, *106-7*, 108
    shoe, making, 107-8, *106-7*,
    108
braid, 33, 36, 46, 60, 80

brocade, 31, 64, 122
broderie Anglaise, *90*, 122
'bump', 32
buttons, 53, 61, *61*, 119, *119*

calico, 64, 93, 122
chair, 70, *71*
    cover, 64
    cushions, *see under* Covers
changing mat, making, 96-7, *96-7*
checks, 9, 13, *23*, 50, *64*, 74, *75*,
    79
chintz, 9, 17, *17*, 25, 31, 64, 122
classical style, 9, 31, 50
coffee tables, 74, 80
colour, 9, 12, 13, *15-17*, *20*, *21*,
    22, *23*, *24*, 25, 26, 31, 32,
    33, 34, *40*, 50, *50*, *51*, 53, 56,
    58, 64, *64*, 74, 77, 78, 84, *84*, 90
contemporary style, 9, *22*, 25, 31,
    50, 64, *65*, 74
contrast, 12, 34, 50, 56, 59, *65*,
    77
coordination, 25, 31, 33, 50, 56,
    77, 84, 90, 107
cord, decorative, 33, 58, 60
    using, 60, *60*
corners, *see* Mitred corners *and
    under* Seams
cot duvet cover, *see under* Covers
cot quilt, *see under* Quilts
cotton, 13, 31, 64, 70, 77, 92, 93,
    94, 122
cotton sateen, 44
country style, *33*, *85*, 70
coverlet, 90, 93
covers
    bolster, making and piping,
    61, *61*
    chair, 64, *119*
    cot duvet, making, 101, *101*
    cushion, 50, *50*
        borders, *see under* Borders
        box, making, 64, 68, 69
        chair, tie-on, piped or frilled,
        making, *62-3*,
        70-1, *70*, *71*
        closings, 53-5, *53-5*, 119
        fabrics, 25, 50, 64
        frills, *see under* Frills
        piping, 56, *66*, 67, 68, 69,
        70, *70*
        round, making, 53, 55, *55*,
        56
        seat, making, 66, 67, *67*
        shapes, 50
        square, making, 53, *53*, 56,
        58, *58*
        trimming, 50, *50*, 53, 56,
        58-61, *58*, *59*, *60*, *61*, 64
    dust, child's, making, *99*, *99*
    duvet, 90, 93, 118
        closings, 92, 101

    making, 92, *92*
    loose, 64
    sofa, 64
curtains, 9, 13, *20*, *23*, 25, 26,
    29, *30*, 31, 32, *32*, 33, *33*,
    40, 42, 44, 50, *51*, 56
    accessories, *see* Pelmets *and*
    Tie-backs
    bed, *20*, 84, 86, *87*
        making, 86, *86*
    bound edges, 32, 33, 34, *34*,
    37, *40*, 86
    dress, 38, *39*
        making, 38, *38*
    headings, *see* Headings
    lined, 36-7, *37*, 42
        making, 36-7, *36-7*, 117
    linings, *see*, Lining
    measuring up, *see under*
    Measuring up
    tie-on, *30*, 34, *35*
        making, 34, *34*
    track, *32*, 44, 46
    trimming, 36, *see also* bound
    edges *above*
curved seams, *see under* Seams
cushions, 12, 26, *50*, *51*, 64, *64*,
    84
    bolster, *20*, 61, *61*, 64, 84
    pads, 53, 61, 67, 68
    see also under Covers

damask, *15*, 31, 74, 80, 122
design, 12, 17, *20-3*, 25
details, *21*, 33, *40*, 90, *90*, *91*
dining rooms, 25
dining tables, 74
drapery, 9, 31, 64
draw-string bags, *see under* Bags
dress curtains, *see under* Curtains
dress table-cloths, *see under*
    Table-cloths
dressing tables, 74
dust covers, *see under* Covers
duvet covers, *see under* Covers

edging, *21*, 33, 50, 58, 59, 74,
    77, 78, 81, *81*
embroidered flat border, *see under*
    Borders
embroidery, 50, *50*, 53, 58, *58*,
    78, *78*, 79
envelope bags, *see under* Bags
ethnic weaves, 13

fabric, 9, 12-13, *14-17*, *20*, *21*,
    22, *24*, 25, *26*, *26*, 27, 31,
    32, 42, 44, 46, 47, 50, 53,
    59, 64, *65*, 74, 77, 80, 84,
    84, 89, 90, 92, 93, 94, 96,
    100, 102, *106-7*, 109, 117,
    118, *see also under names
    of fabrics, items of soft*

    furnishing
fabric-covered boxes, *see under*
    Boxes
fabric glue, using, 108
fabric ties, *see* Ties, fabric
fastenings, 119, *see also projects
    for applications*
festoon blinds, *23*, 31, 46-7, *46*
    making, 47, *47*
    tracks, 47
flat double border, making, *see
    under* Borders
flat seam, *see under* Seams
florals, 9, 13, 25, 31, 50, 74, *74*,
    79, 84
flowers, *14*, *17*, 74
formal table-cloths, *see under*
    Table-cloths
French seam, *see under* Seams
frilled tie-on chair cover, *see under*
    Covers
frills, 33, 46, 50, 58, 59, *59*, 71,
    90, *121*
    bound-edge, making, 59, *59*
    double, 59, 121, *121*
    frills on frills, 59
    single, 59, *59*, 121, *121*
    tie-on chair cushion cover, *see
    under* Covers
    trimming, 59, *59*
fringing, *21*, *40*, 33, 36, 46, *51*,
    53, 58, 60, *60*, 77, *77*, 78,
    112

gathered-end bolster, 61, *61*
geometric prints, 9, 13, 25, 31, 64
gimp, 33, 36
gingham, 70, 77, 122
glue, fabric, *see* Fabric glue

hanger
    padded child's, 99, *99*
    picture, *see* Picture hanger
hat box, *see under* Boxes
headings, 31, *32*
    bows, 31
    loops, 31
    tape, 31, 32, 36, 44, 46, 47
    ties, 31
        making, 34, *34*
heat-resistant mats, making, 78
hems, 77, 78, 117, *see also under*
    Stitches
herringbone stitch, *see under*
    Stitches
high-tech style, 25
historical style, *20*, 84

inspiration, *10-11*, 12, *14-15*,
    18-19, 20
interfacing, 36, 86, 122
interlining, 32, 117, 122

kelims, 53, 74
kitchens, 70

lace, 13, *23*, 31, 32, 53, 60, 74, 90, *90*, 122
lined curtains, *see under* Curtains
linen, 13
liner for Moses basket, *see* Moses basket, liner for
lining, 31, 32-3, 34, 36, 38, 44, 46, 50, 80, 86, 109, 112, 117, *see also under* Curtains
living rooms, 25
locking stitch, *see under* Stitches

machine
    quilting, *see* Quilting
    satin stitch, *see under* Stitches
mattress ticking, 64, 122
measuring up
    for basic draw-string bag, 112
    for bed curtains, 86
    for bound-edge tie-backs, 40
    for changing mat, 96
    for cot duvet cover, 101
    for cot quilt, 102
    for curtain headings, 32
    for dress curtains, 38
    for duvet cover, 92
    for fabric-covered boxes, 107
    for festoon blind, 47
    for formal table-cloths, 80
    for frilled tie-on cushion cover, 71
    for frills, 59
    for fringed table linen, 77
    for gathered-end bolster cover, 61
    for lined curtains, 36
    for liner for Moses basket, 94
    for nappy or towel holder, 98
    for padded child's hanger, 99
    for pelmet, 38
    for picture hanger, 109
    for pillowcases, 90
    for piped box cushion cover, 68
    for piped cushion cover, 56
    for piped-edge tie-backs, 41
    for piped flat-ended bolster cover, 61
    for piped tie-on chair cushion cover, 70
    for ready-made trimmings, 60
    for reversible quilt, 89
    for Roman blind, 45
    for round cushion covers, 55
    for simple seat cushion, 67
    for simple table linen, 77, 78
    for simple tie blind, 42
    for square cushion covers, 53
    for tie-on curtains, 34
    for valance, 93
minimalist style, 25
mitred corners, 58, 81, 89, 103
Moses basket, liner for, making, 94-5, *94, 95, 97*
muslin, 13, 21, 31, 122

napkins, 74, *75*, 76
    making, 77, *77*, 78, *78*
nappy or towel holder, making 98, *98, 99*
neatening raw edges, 118, *118*
nursery, 94-103, *95, 97, 99, 103*
    accessories, *see* Baby towel, Changing mat, Hangers, Moses basket, liner for, Nappy or towel holder *and under* Covers *and* Quilts

occasional tables, 74, 80
oversewing, 118

paisley, 64
patchwork, machine, 102
pattern, 9, 12, 13, *14-15, 16-17, 24,* 25, 26, *32, 33,* 34, 44, 50, 64, 74, 77, 89, 90, 102, 116
    making, 38, 41, 55, 96, 110, 112
    mixing, 9, *20,* 25
    see also Abstract designs, Checks, Ethnic weaves, Florals, Geometric prints, Gingham, Stripes
pelmets, 9, 13, *23,* 31, *32,* 33, *39*
    making, 38, *38*
period style, 9, *20, 21,* 31, 46, 50, 58, 60, *60,* 74
picture hanger, making, 109, *109*
pillowcases, making, 90-1, *90-1,* 118
    borders, 90, *91*
    edgings, 90, *90, 91*
pinking, 59, 118
piped box cushion, *see under* Covers
piped flat-ended bolster, *see under* Covers
piping, 9, 25, 26, 41, 50, 58, 59, 64, *64,* 67, *67,* 112, 118, 121, *121*
    inserting, 121
    joining, 121
    making, 121
    see also under Covers
polyester/cotton sheeting, 92
press fasteners, 92, 119, *119*
press fastener tape, 92, 119, *119*
proportion, 25, 26

quilting, machine, *88,* 89, *89,* 94, 102, 117
    foot, 117
    guide, 117
quilts, 64, 74, 84, *88*
    cot, making, 102-3, *102, 103*
    reversible, making, 89, *89*

ready-made trimmings, 60, *60, see also* Trimmings
reversible quilt, *see under* Quilts
    ribbon, 34, 42, 60, 80, 90,
109, 120
    mitring edging, 81
roller blinds, 31
    stiffener, 107, 108
Roman blinds, 25, 31, 32
    making, 44-5, *44, 45*
rosettes, 46, 109
round cushion covers, *see under* Covers

sample boards, 25, 26, *26, 27*
sateen, 31, 122
satin, 64, 122
satin stitch, machine, *see under* Stitches
seams
    corners, 118, *118*
    curved, 118, *118*
    flat, 89, 118, *118*
    French, 59, 91, 92, 93, 101, 109, 118, *118*
    mitred, 58, 81, *81,* 89, 103
seating, 61, *61,* 64, *64, 65, 66, see also* Chair, Covers *and* Cushions
shoe box, *see under* Boxes
silk, 13, 109
simple table linen, *76,* 77
    edging, 78, *78, 79*
    making, 77, 78
simple tie blind, making, 42, *42-3*
simple seat cushion, *see under* Covers
sloping blinds, *33*
sofas, 13, 25, 26, 50, 64, 67, 84
    square cushion covers, *see under* Covers
stitches, 116-7, *116*
    back stitch, 116, *116*
    hemming, 116, *116,* 117
    herringbone, 36, 89, 116, *116*
    ladder stitch, 116, *116*
    locking stitch, 36, 117, *117*
    quilting, machine, *88,* 89, *89*
    running, 89, 117, *117*
    satin, machine, 58, 59, 77, 78
    slip, 117, *117*
    tacking, 89, 93, 102, 116, 117, *117,* 118
    zigzag, machine, 93, 118
stools, *65*
storage, 84, 110, 112
stripes, 9, *20,* 25, 44, 50, 64, 89
    styles, 9
swags, 33

table-cloths, 12, 74, *74, 76*
    formal, or, dress decorative, making, 80, 81, *81* lined with bound edges, making, 80, *80*
    simple, making, 77, *77,* 78
table linen, *see* Napkins, Simple table linen, Table-cloths *and* Table-mats
table-mats, 25, 74, *74, 75*
    heat-resistant, making, 78
    making, 77, *77,* 78

tables, *see type*
tape, 34, 42, *see also* Press fastener tape *and under* Headings
tassels, *21,* 33, 61
textures, 9, 12, 13, 17, *17,* 50, 64, 74, 84
throws, 64, *64,* 84
tie-backs, 9, 13, 31, 33, 36, 40, *40*
    bound-edge, making, 40, *40, 41, 41*
    piped-edge tie-backs, making, 41, *41*
tie-blind, 32
tie-on chair cushions, *see under* Covers
tie-on curtains, *see under* Curtains
    ties, fabric, *30,* 31, 32, 33, 34, *34, 35, 71,* 90, 92
    making, 34, *34,* 42, 70, *70,* 86, 94, 97, 98, 101, 111,
towelling, 96, 100
towel
    holder, nappy or, *see* Nappy or towel holder
    baby, *see* Baby towel
tracks, *see under* Austrian blinds *and* Curtains
traditional style, 9, 13, 31, 58, 60, *60,* 109, *109*
trimmings, *21,* 31, 33, 36, 40, 46, *46,* 50, *50,* 58, *58,* 60, *60,* 90, *90,* 120, *120, see also* Binding, Borders, Bows, Braid, *Broderie Anglaise,* Cord, decorative, Edging, Embroidery, Fringing, Frills, Gimp, Lace, Piping *and* Tassels *and under* Covers
    tweed, 53

under-curtains, 31
upholstery, 9, 13, *20,* 25, 50, *50,* 56, 64

valance, making, 93, *93*
Velcro, 32
    using, 42, 92, 119
    spots, using, 53
velvet, 53, 109
vent openings, making, 54

wadding, 89, 94, 99, 102, 122
wall-to-wall curtains, *33*
wicker furniture, 67, 68, *69*
windows, *28-9,* 29-47, *30, 32, 33, 37, 40, 44, 46*
window seat, *64*
wools, 31

zigzag, machine, *see under* Stitches
zips, 92
    inserting, 54, *54,* 55, *55, 119*

Acknowledgments

The publisher would like to thank the following photographers and organizations for their kind permission to reproduce the photographs in this book:

1 Designers Guild (David Montgomery); 2 Conran Octopus (styled by Jo Willer); 3 Designers Guild (David Montgomery); 6-7 Designers Guild (David Montgomery); 10 *above left* Carlos Navajas; 10 *above right* Designers Guild (David Montgomery); 10 *centre left* Designers Guild (David Montgomery); 10 *centre right* Carlos Navajas; 10 *below left* Iliona/Agence Top; 10 *below right* Designers Guild (David Montgomery); 11 *above left* Guy Bouchet; 11 *above right* Designers Guild (David Montgomery); 11 *centre left* Designers Guild (David Montgomery); 11 *centre right* Carlos Navajas; 11 *below left* Designers Guild (David Montgomery); 11 *below right* Hussenot/Agence Top; 14 *top* Mazin/Agence Top; 14 *above* Designers Guild (David Montgomery); 14 *centre* George Wright; 14 *below* Designers Guild (David Montgomery; 14-15 *top* Designers Guild (David Montgomery); 14-15 *above* Carlos Navajas; 14-15 *centre* Designers Guild (David Montgomery); 14-15 *below* S & O Mathews; 15 *top* Photograph by Gilles de Chabaneix, from *Greek Style* by Suzanne Slesin, Stafford Cliff and Daniel Rozensztroch (Thames & Hudson); 15 *above* Designers Guild (David Montgomery); 15 *centre* S & O Mathews; 15 *below* Designers Guild (David Montgomery); 16 *top* George Wright; 16 *above* Carlos Navajas; 16 *centre* Designers Guild (David Montgomery); 16 *below* Carlos Navajas; 16-17 *top* Richard Bryant/Arcaid; 16-17 *above* Designers Guild (David Montgomery); 16-17 *centre* Carlos Navajas; 16-17 *below* Designers Guild (David Montgomery); 17 *top* Designers Guild (David Montgomery); 17 *above* Susan Witney; 17 *centre* Designers Guild (David Montgomery); 17 *below* Carlos Navajas; 18 *above left* Guy Bouchet/Conran Octopus; 18 *above right* Carlos Navajas; 18 *centre and below* Carlos Navajas; 19 *above left* Reichel/Agence Top; 19 *above right* Carlos Navajas; 19 *centre left* George Wright; 19 *centre right* Carlos Navajas; 19 *below left* Gilles de Chabaneix; 19 *below right* Mike England; 20 *above* Victoria & Albert Museum, London/Bridgeman Art Library; 20 *below* Fritz von der Schulenburg (Karl Lagerfeld); 21 *above left and right* Guy Bouchet; 21 *below* left Sotheby's, London; 22 *left* Derry Moore; 22 *right* Richard Bryant/Arcaid; 23 *above left* Lars Hallen; 23 *below left* Photograph by Gilles de Chabaneix, from *Greek Style* by Suzanne Slesin; Stafford Cliff and Daniel Rozensztroch (Thames & Hudson); 23 *right* Bergen Kommune/Bridgeman Art Library; 24 Designers Guild (David Montgomery); 26-7 Conran Octopus (styled by Jo Willer); 28-32 Designers Guild (David Montgomery); 33 *above and centre* Designers Guild (David Montgomery); 35-7 Designers Guild (David Montgomery); 40-3 Designers Guild (David Montgomery); 44 David Montgomery/Conran Octopus; 46 Derry Moore; 48-52 Designers Guild (David Montgomery); 57-9 Designers Guild (David Montgomery); 61-4 Designers Guild (David Montgomery); 65 *above* Designers Guild (David Montgomery); 65 *below left* Maison de Marie Claire/Dhar/Pelle; 65 *below right* Country Living (David Montgomery); 66-71 Designers Guild (David Montgomery); 74-5 World Press Network/IPC Magazines; 82-3 Designers Guild (David Montgomery); 84 *above* Designers Guild (David Montgomery); 84 *below* Designers Guild (Simon Brown); 85-7 Designers Guild (David Montgomery); 88 Designers Guild (Simon Brown); 90 Vogue Living (George Seper); 91-2 Designers Guild (David Montgomery); 103 Designers Guild (Simon Brown).

The following photographs were specially taken for Conran Octopus by David Montgomery: 8 *above right* 33 *below*, 60, 72-3, 76-7, 78-81, 95-99, 104-115.